PARENTING TWEENS & TEENS

HOW TO RAISE HEALTHY HUMANS WITH CHARACTER

GALEN COLE, PH.D.

PARENTING tweens & TEENS How to Raise Healthy Humans With Character

© Copyright, 2022, Dr. Galen E. Cole

All rights reserved. No part of this book may be reproduced or transmitted in any form or by any means, electronic or mechanical, including photocopying, or recording, or by any information storage and retrieval system, without the written permission of the publisher, except where permitted by law.

Printed in the USA.

First Edition

Although the author and publisher have made every effort to ensure the accuracy and completeness of the information contained in this book, we assume no responsibility for errors, inaccuracies, omissions, or inconsistencies herein. Any slights of people, places, or organizations are unintentional.

ACKNOWLEDGMENTS

Priscilla Wolfe and I were young, in love, almost penniless, had very little education, lived a thousand miles away from our families and decided to get married and have a large family…what could go wrong? What's hilarious is that we actually thought we could make it…and make it we did. This August 18 we celebrate 47 years together.

When we started we both went to school and worked and somewhere along the way we had 5 children who are grown adults — Amanda, Zachary, Nicholes, Joshua and Jordan. And then, just as we thought we were empty nesters, a young girl showed up who needed a home. It only took my wife saying "remember, she only gets one childhood" to convince me that we should take on raising Lilly Rose.

All told, Priscilla and I have been faithful parenting partners who have "been there and done that" when it comes to parenting. This book represents some of the many approaches we have taken to raise what most of the people who know us agree are some of the most amazing adults on the planet. To my wife Priscilla, I acknowledge that you did the bulk of the heavy lifting. Thank you for your tireless efforts in raising 6 healthy humans with character!

INTRODUCTION

Parenting can be immensely satisfying, but I think it's safe to say it is never easy. There are aspects that are instinctive, but that doesn't mean parenting is always logical. And although the intensity of parenting comes and goes through phases of a child's life, most conscientious parents would agree the task never ends – nor would they want it any other way. Parenting is a lifetime no-cut contract.

Because the reality is "once a parent, always a parent", it is important to learn how to enjoy the ride when you embark on this treacherous and adventure-filled road – from my perspective, nothing can be more worthwhile.

Having co-parented five children with my wife, Priscilla, I can honestly say, "I've been there and done that", when it comes to experiencing firsthand what it is like to take an infant home from the hospital and then raise that child to adulthood. As I reflect, the most challenging times to determine a path forward were when my children were ages 11 to 18 — tweens and teens. Because I took parenting very seriously and struggled terribly with my first teen, I decided to write a book about what I believe 'works' when it comes to raising children, with a focus on navigating the tween and teen years. I started this book when my children were young, and updated it multiple times as my knowledge, skills, parenting abilities, and multiple trial and error scenarios evolved.

There are some people in this world who have been 'self-taught'. They have learned to navigate life without good parenting, and overcome scores of obstacles through sheer determination and internal grit. Some of these children even miraculously thrive despite little or no parenting. It is important to keep in mind such children are the exception, not the rule. Intentional and purposeful parenting will always be a gift for your children. They will be much more likely to be equipped to face life's challenges with responsibility, confidence, and poise if you are committed from the outset to help them develop a strong identity.

Parenting is the oldest job in history. Countless books have been written on the topic; it can be difficult to know where to turn. My approach, after more than three decades as a father and family psychotherapist, is that logical, consequence-based strategies focusing on shaping a child's character, rather than simply changing his or her behavior, are the most effective.

As I tell all my family therapy clients who are struggling with parenting issues, I believe effective parenting is about creating a vision that outlines how they plan to shape future adults. With this in mind, it takes more than love and commitment to maintain a healthy, loving relationship that withstands the test of time. To raise healthy kids with character, you need to help them capture a vision for their own lives that goes beyond just survival in a world growing increasingly complicated and difficult to navigate.

I have based my approach on the most prominent, evidence-based approaches to parenting I could find – some are cutting edge, and some have withstood the test of time. These include "Parenting with Love and Logic" by Foster Cline and Jim Fay, "Positive Parenting with a Plan" by Dr. Matthew Johnson, "Raising Great Kids" and "Boundaries with Kids", both by Dr. Henry Cloud and Dr. John Townsend. What's included here around character and sex education was influenced by the research and teachings of Dr. Stan Weed, who accompanied me on a trip through China where we both conducted formative research and trainings aimed at helping parents, teachers, and leaders improve their efforts to teach and reinforce positive character traits.

More recently, a Harvard study turned parenting book provided eye-opening insights into successful parenting. The result? The Formula: Unlocking the Secrets to Raising Highly Successful Children. This study interviewed a great number of highly successful people – and their parents – to unlock the keys to their success. What unfolded was an evolution of parenting roles that transform as the child grows. At the core of these successful parents was a burning desire to do just that: be successful parents. Let us begin our journey to the same goal.

1
A BRIEF INTRO TO THE ADOLESCENT MIND

THE FOUNDATION TO SUCCESS IN MOST THINGS LIES IN KNOWING WHAT you're up against. There are many developmental changes that occur as your children enter the tween and teen years, and these changes require adjustments to your parenting approach. The following is a list of ways the adolescent mind is shifting and changing during these years, and how parents can adjust.

They are developing an identity. This pursuit comes with a host of changes: a lack of interest in things they once enjoyed (such as play or hobbies), a more sensitive self-consciousness, and a host of self-doubt. Often their anger and lashing out comes from being generally unsure of who they are, not necessarily because they're ungrateful for your love. This can be a beautiful process, if you can see beyond the day to day, but it is almost always wrought with challenges.

They are going through many physical changes. This requires patience and respect on the part of the parents. Hormonal changes are happening faster than your kids even realize, and much of their behavior puzzles them as well. This is a breeding ground for many difficult conversations, but you can set yourself up for success by leading with questions. Rather than shocking them with unsolicited science lessons. Ask them what they already know before assuming they don't, when it comes to those uncomfortable-for-everyone conversations.

When you feel awkward, just embrace it. If it were easy, there wouldn't be so many books written about it!

They want to be seen as independent persons. You might find your teen grows highly frustrated when you tell them something they 'already know'. During this time, it is helpful to transition into doing more listening and less unsolicited teaching and/or lecturing. The years are coming when your children will actually be on their own, and the earlier you learn to transition from director to coach/advisor, the smoother that transition will be.

They value their privacy. This can be a hot issue when it comes to parenting teens, but understand their desire for privacy isn't all bad – it's all a part of differentiating themselves from their family of origin. If you start off with an attitude of trust and with clear expectations of the consequences of breaking that trust, you'll start out on the right foot with your teen.

They still depend on you. The ways your children depend on you will evolve as they grow, but they still depend on you, believe it or not, and despite protestations to the contrary. Be dependable. Show up, keep your promises, and maintain your family rhythms. As they explore the world more and more (both figuratively and literally), make sure they always have a predictable, safe place to land. Starting healthy family rhythms earlier in your children's lives (as we will talk in detail in this book) helps you to establish natural scenarios that encourage your kids to be open and share what's going on in their lives.

If you wait until they're older teens to implement some of these things, it will feel a great deal more like you're 'prying' into their lives, rather than simply doing what you've always done to show interest.

When children are younger, the vision comes almost exclusively from you as a parent. Being specific about the qualities you want to see expressed in your child, as early as possible, will give you the best chance of actually achieving these goals. As the child matures, you begin to share more of that responsibility with them as they create a vision for their own lives. We've always told our children, "We don't want you to be like most people. Most people don't set goals and attain them. Most people are not conscientious when it comes to caring for their bodies. Most people don't have a vision for their lives. Live beyond what you see around you!"

Once again, what's included here is not just theoretical fun and games. I've based my techniques on the best research that's out there, combined it with over 20 years' experience as a psychotherapist focused on family issues, and equally many years as a parent. Successfully, hopefully, coparenting six children with my wife didn't hurt either!

2

UNDERSTANDING CHARACTER TRAITS

A POPULAR BIBLICAL PROVERB STATES, "WHERE THERE IS NO VISION, the people perish." As a psychotherapist, I often refer to this ancient wisdom to emphasize the importance of creating a vision as an essential part of a parenting plan. From my point of view, without a plan or vision, parents are doomed to unnecessary stress and headache as they wander aimlessly in their attempts to parent. Children are walking, living, and breathing vehicles of **chaos**. If you don't have a clear and positive picture of what you want your child to become, combined with an effective way to support that vision, the result can be disappointing, and could even contribute to some of the greatest regrets in your life.

You can envision your child's future in many ways, two of which are very common. One way has to do with who they are as a person – the qualities and characteristics that define them as individuals. The other is in terms of their accomplishments and status in life – a noted musician, successful doctor or lawyer, famous sports figure, a business tycoon, or any number of worthwhile occupations that represent "success". Those accomplishments all have the potential to be good things. You would not, however, take pride in your child's accomplishments and status if he/she had to cheat, lie, and steal to get there. Nor would you be proud if upon reaching their chosen position in life, they acted in that position without honor, respect, compassion, fairness, or integrity. We have all seen too many examples of 'successful' people who have abused their positions of trust and stature to take unfair advantage, to manipulate, to abuse, and to cover up.

Thinking about our child's future in terms of who they are as a person – the qualities and characteristics that define them as individuals – offers an important vision and definition of success. If you don't begin with a vision of who they will be, rather than what they will do, you will find it very difficult to effectively determine how to use your family's greatest commodity – your time – to shape your children into the people you, and they, would like them to become. "Character, in the long run, is the decisive factor in the life of an individual and of nations alike," reminds Theodore Roosevelt.

It is important to remind you while you are 'in charge', this is a cooperative project. You will not be able to 'mold' a child into what you want, and you shouldn't, unless you have buy-in from the child. For example, if you want your son to have a 'normal' haircut, and he wants to keep long hair, you may win the battle at the barber, but you will lose the war of getting buy-in on even more important issues. Of course, health, safety, and honesty issues are non-negotiable, but everything else has some wiggle room… intend to use it judiciously.

It is one thing to vaguely agree, of course, we want our children to 'be good', or to 'have good character' – but we are much more likely to see a positive outcome if we think in more specific terms. "Treat others with consideration and respect, be fair and honest in all of your dealings, do your best in all your pursuits, etc.," will give us a much stronger starting point in developing a plan for their success and wholeness as human beings. The more specifically we envision those qualities and characteristics, the more likely we are to increase our chances of fostering them in our children.

While there are numerous qualities that could be identified as valuable and desirable, I will focus on a manageable set of "universal" traits that provide a critical foundation for a child's character. I call them universal because they apply across cultures, time periods, racial and ethnic groups, and belief systems. By manageable, I mean a numbered set of character qualities and personal skills that can be taught by parents without the key concepts becoming lost in an endless list of possibilities. This process is supposed to help you zero in and focus, not cause you to become so overwhelmed you can't follow through with these commitments. This education process is not quick, and not easy. Oftentimes the most important things in life aren't. But the good news is, it can be done.

Simply using a search engine to identify 'character traits' yields many different examples of healthy character traits (one of thousands of examples is here https://afineparent.com/building-character/good-character-traits.html) that all parents can aspire to inculcate in their children as they socialize them toward becoming knowledgeable, skilled, capable adults who are imbued with character traits required to live safe, productive, healthy and happy lives.

Albert Einstein said, "The most important human endeavor is the striving for morality in our actions. Our inner balance and even our very existence depend on it. Only morality in our actions can give beauty and dignity to life."

3

KEY CHARACTER QUALITIES

You can also begin by reflecting on the following list, where I have described each trait as well as how (ideally!) the young person would interpret it, and apply it to their lives. This is my list and I am sure you have a list that includes other traits, and may delete some of mine as not as important. Keep in mind you can become as detailed or as minimal as your parenting style is comfortable, but this list is fairly comprehensive and can get us started.

1. *Humility.* A humble person does not see themselves more highly than they see another person. They do not believe they have all the answers. Teaching children humility is teaching them they are not better than others.

The child's response: I have great and irreplaceable value, but no more value than others. I can speak confidently about the things I know, but should never speak down to another person.

2. *Gratitude & Contentment.* A grateful and content person recognizes the gifts they have received in life and focuses their

heart on being thankful for those things, rather than endlessly focusing on what they do not have.

The child's response: I am incredibly fortunate to have what I have in relationships, material things, and natural talents and abilities. Everything in my life is a gift, and I don't want to waste my time being discontent. Whatever it is I seem to be discontent with, I can either let it go, or find a way to work to earn it.

3. *Compassion & Empathy*. Compassionate and empathetic people are interested in the difficulties others face and seek to find solutions to them. They are active listeners.

The child's response: The thoughts and feelings of others are important to me. Rather than always just being focused on what concerns me, I will listen to others in such a way I can understand what they are going through and support them in any way possible.

4. *Industriousness & Hard Work*. Industrious and hardworking people are committed to following through with the tasks they have taken on, whether these tasks have been assigned to them, or are the result of pursuing a passion. They recognize life's true enjoyment comes from honestly earning your rewards, financial, psychic, or otherwise.

The child's response: I will devote my energies to working hard at the things I love and the things that are my responsibility to do. I understand my hard work reflects on who I am, and I will not cut corners in ways that cause other people to work harder to make up for my laziness.

5. *Courage*. Courageous people take on challenges despite their fear, from a commitment to personal growth or sacrifice.

The child's response: I will do things that scare me because I do not want to be conquered by fear.

6. *Honesty & Integrity*. Honest people with integrity don't keep secrets or remain invulnerable – what you see is what you get. They possess the same character in all environments such as work, school, home, etc.

The child's response: I will remain true to who I am and will not cheat, steal, or lie to get something I want.

7. *Generosity*. Generous people share their wealth with those around them. They do not hoard out of fear, but consider the things they have been given as gifts that should be shared.

The child's response: I will freely share the things I have been given. Giving brings me joy because I know I have the opportunity to serve someone else.

8. *Patience*. Patient people recognize what is unfolding around them is bigger than their immediate needs. They're able to see themselves as a part of a grander story instead of the star of the show.

The child's response: I will recognize my needs are only one piece of the puzzle, and will gladly wait and accommodate for others, understanding the world doesn't revolve around me.

9. *Self-control*. Self-controlled people realize it is possible to have too much of a good thing. They can effectively moderate life's pleasures and take responsibility for their actions and decisions.

The child's response: Just because I like something doesn't mean I need to indulge in unlimited amounts. I recognize I am responsible for my own decisions and will choose not to blame any of my decisions on "I couldn't help myself".

· · ·

10. *Adaptability*. Adaptable people are able to pivot when unexpected circumstances arise. They don't get bent out of shape when things don't go as planned.
The child's response: I recognize that life is not predictable. When challenges arise, I will move into problem-solving mode rather than throwing a fit.

11. *Optimism*. Optimistic people grab on to the positive when they are faced with challenges. They do not waste time with self-pity or despair but find ways to make their situation better.
The child's response: When I unexpectedly face a disappointment I cannot change, I will do what I can to adjust my expectations and find the 'bright side' of my new circumstance.

12. *Respect*. Respectful people understand appropriate social boundaries and treat people with kindness.
The child's response: I will treat both adults and my peers as though they have worth and value.

13. *Accountability*. Accountable people reject a victim mentality and take responsibility for the decisions they make.
The child's response: I refuse to play the blame game – when I make a decision, I will own that decision and its consequences and not try to skirt my responsibility.

14. *Agency/Initiative*. Initiators take it upon themselves to create reasonable solutions for the problems they see. They have a belief in their own abilities and don't wait for others to act.
The child's response: I believe I have the skills, gifts, and talents to solve my own problems and make a positive impact on the

world around me. Seeking help when I need it, I will take it upon myself to contribute wherever I can.

15. *Critical Thinking*: Critical thinking is the process of looking beyond the surface of information and seeking out its true meaning. Critical thinkers can weigh pros and cons and consider alternative perspectives when making important decisions.
Implication for the child: I can learn to ask valuable questions that help me understand and develop a worldview based on beliefs I have carefully considered and questioned in great depth.

16. *Goal Setting:* Goal setting is planning and preparing for the future by setting out the path one will follow. It involves both long-term and short-term goals, and includes both the character traits I strive for as well as my accomplishments.
Implication for the child: I can decide what I want to accomplish in my life, and the kind of person I want to become. I can take steps now that will put me on the path to achieving those goals.

17. *Coping with Peer Pressure*: Peer pressure is the influence others attempt to inflict on their peers to receive a desired outcome. It can be positive, negative, or both. Coping with peer pressure means being able to compare your own standards of right and wrong with what others think and feel. It means having the courage to act according to one's own standards, regardless of what others do or say.
Implication for the child: I know what I stand for, and I will act according to my own standards regardless of what others do or say. The principles and standards I am learning will be my guide to making good decisions rather than my peers. I will look for friends who are making good decisions and who support my good choices.

· · ·

18. *Conflict Resolution*: Conflict resolution is the ability to solve problems by communicating, negotiating, and compromising without going against the ethical principles and standards one has learned and committed to.

Implication for the child: I am capable of solving problems. I can communicate, negotiate, and compromise without going against my own standards. I can recognize the worth and rights of others, and that I do not always have to have my own way. By sharing my own feelings, and understanding and respecting how others feel, I will be better prepared to resolve conflicts.

4

FOCUSING ON KEY CHARACTER TRAITS - EXERCISE

While all these traits are important, as I mentioned earlier, trying to focus on all of them at once is an exercise in futility. Parenting is about the long game, and it takes place in many movements and seasons. You will get the best result if you start with small, attainable goals, and narrow your focus where it can best be used. Since you're reading this book about parenting tweens and teens, you likely have at least one child who is older and whom you've had a chance to get to know. Your specific child comes with his/her own set of strengths and weaknesses that have come partially from natural wiring and partially from the way you have nurtured him/her. Though you want them to exhibit all the universally positive character traits, you can use the following list of questions to bring to light which of these traits warrant your most immediate attention.

Initially, it may make sense to choose three character traits that cover different aspects of the child's life. For instance, being hardworking and exercising grit are similar, while being hardworking and compassionate cover multiple areas. Whatever traits you choose should be consistent with your most highly held values.

Think of the last three battles you had with your child. Was there a theme? Think about what character trait lies at the root of the issue you were having. If they were refusing to clean their room, there could be multiple character traits at play. Seek to understand whether the issue was laziness, disrespect, or disorganization. It is important to stay focused on the 'why' that comes from their character rather than simply getting their behavior to match your expectations. So, we are seeking to help change/mold the character rather than just getting compliance with a rule or expectation.

Think about the last time you were surprised and disappointed at how your child behaved. Maybe you saw them treat a sibling with disrespect, or learned about a way they got into trouble at school. What character traits might need to be strengthened in order to empower them to make a better choice next time?

Is there a situation you commonly "rescue" your child from because you don't want them to fail or suffer? What ways might you routinely get in the way of their building character because of the way you project your own past hurts or insecurities on their lives? Related character traits here could be initiative, courage, or commitment. Yes, you want to protect them from real injury, but risk is something they are going to have to learn (character trait) to assess and take or refuse.

Look at the list of character traits and think about any you haven't had the opportunity to observe in your child. Are your children committed to things with which they have to follow through? Are they being challenged to do things that scare them? Are they given opportunities to demonstrate their generosity?

After you have had a chance to reflect on these questions and select the three character traits you'd like to focus on, complete the following exercise to solidify your decision.

FOCUSING ON KEY CHARACTER TRAITS – EXERCISE

In the first column, write the trait you're planning to focus on.

In the second column, provide a brief explanation of why that trait came to mind. If it's worth doing, it's worth knowing why you're doing it!

In the third column, write a sentence that describes something your child would do or say to demonstrate to you they have internalized the trait.

In the fourth column, start to brainstorm some actionable steps you could take toward achieving these character goals. The rest of this book will go into further detail about how to make a parenting plan that supports your goal, but this exercise is just to get you thinking. You will see teaching about the character trait exists on each row in the "actionable steps" column.

Character Trait	Your "Why"	A "Visual" Goal	Actionable Steps
Generosity	I was surprised by the way my child refused to share with their siblings.	My child would notice something their sibling needed and voluntarily go out of their way to share what they had with them.	Teaching about generosity. Asking questions about opportunities the child had to be generous – maybe ones they missed, maybe ones they took. Giving a child extra funds to creatively use to give someone else joy or give to a charity they choose and care about.
Patience	Three times this week my child has grown excessively impatient and has treated others poorly as a result or thrown fits.	My child would respond calmly with a statement like, "Ok, no problem," when learning that something they were looking forward to had to be delayed.	Teaching about patience. Giving the child opportunity to save money in order to purchase something they want. Deliberately challenging your child's patience and delaying something they anticipate.
Initiative	I've realized that I don't encourage my child to take initiative – I usually start things for them or just let them do what they've always done.	My child would come up with their own idea about how to solve a problem in the household, their own life, or the world and take steps toward solving it.	Teaching about initiative. Providing a "challenge" to your child to initiate a solution to something that's been bothering them. Provide support and reward for doing so.

This is no accident – there are many ways to discretely instill these character traits in your children through natural consequences to their actions, etc., but that does not negate the importance of back-and-forth open discussion with your children about these items. Again, get the 'buy-in', solidify the trait; don't just get compliance.

5

QUALITIES OF EFFECTIVE PARENTS

Life is a journey – on it, we never stop learning. Just as you want your children to possess the character traits that will later be critical to their success and value systems as human beings, so we, as parents, are also on a continual growth process toward becoming the people we want to be. As the adage says, "more is caught than is taught". Our modeling of the behaviors we want our children to copy is an irreplaceable ingredient to this process. If your children see *you* putting in the effort to make changes, persevere toward an important goal, ask for forgiveness, and keep learning, they might just be inspired to do the same.

Parenting is a process that involves both skill and love. Parents who believe they can get by with simply an instinctual desire to love and want what's best for their child may quickly find themselves in over their heads. Love is necessary for good parenting, but it's not sufficient. Parenting has been done in villages since the first generations – no one was designed to do it alone.

This book is just a 21st century representation of passing on this wisdom. You might love the game of baseball and love your teammates, but that's not going to win you any games. Your skill, practice, and execution are going to be the magic ingredients to your success.

It's ok, we can say it out loud. Some people have an easier time parenting than others. It may be due to their disposition, their own upbringing, or even the amount of time they're able to devote to the process. That is not an indication they love their children more than those who need more education or support. Reaching out for that support and putting in the hard effort to do parenting well is the best gift you can give your children.

Find the best ways for you to learn and pour your efforts into those. Some people get excited about the idea of reading many books; others would rather avoid them at all costs. Committing yourself to a mentor or an accountability partner can be a great way to keep yourself on track and keep your skills sharp. Others can pour courage into you when you feel like giving up. They can share tips and tricks you haven't thought of yet. They can team up with you as another healthy adult to invest in your child's life.

If you're parenting as a team, make a regular effort to be on the same page with your partner. If possible, this is not something that should be left only to real-time conflict resolution. This means having the occasional or regular meeting to discuss how things are going, issues that might have come up since the last meeting, or issues being brought up by the children. You have to make decisions as to how you will handle or pursue certain subjects. Then, when it is time, you aren't scrambling to show a united front in terms of your decisions as the parents.

The most successful parents actively and openly communicate together about their parenting goals with one another and are willing to hear input from the "other side". Discover each of your strengths and use them to your advantage. Most importantly, make a decision and stay unified.

There will be times it will not be possible to pursue unity with your parenting partner, such as difficult cases of divorce or challenged marriages. Do not let the personal challenges you face discourage you from being committed to instilling positive character traits in your children. Do what you can to get yourself healthy, rise above the challenges you're facing, and stay focused and present for your children.

6

DEVELOPING A FAMILY MANAGEMENT PLAN

ONE OF A PARENT'S MAIN RESPONSIBILITIES IS KEEPING THE PEACE. And that doesn't just mean keeping everyone from killing each other. A peaceful kingdom is one where all the citizens know their roles and do what they can to take care of each other. They aren't constantly vying for positions of power, they aren't at war, and they aren't confused about what they're supposed to be doing and when. Not only that, but they are also glad to fulfill their responsibilities for the good of all. If you already have teenagers (or even just toddlers), that probably sounds like a pretty lofty goal for a household, but remember, a goal is just that – a goal.

A defining characteristic of a functional family is the presence of order in the home. The opposite is also true – dysfunctional families are typically characterized by chaos and disorder. Though it is likely that the phrase "one man's order is another' chaos," does immediately come to mind. One of the greatest ways you can move away from chaos and towards a peaceful home is to actually develop parenting strategies rather than simply "shooting from the hip". Remember: effective parenting does *not* always come naturally, it's *rarely* easy, and it *can* be learned.

The parenting strategy outlined in this section of the book

describes how you can develop a Family Management Plan and includes guidance on how to (again, any or all):

1. develop family goals and a goal statement,
2. decide which activities family members will engage in to achieve these goals,
3. set rules to support goals and activities,
4. justify rules,
5. select, assign, and administer appropriate consequences,
6. administer discipline appropriately,
7. motivate compliance with family rules,
8. contract for performance when motivating is lacking,
9. evaluate performance, and
10. develop and maintain a healthy relationship with each child.

The first step in effectively managing your family is simple, but critical. Put together a notebook that will eventually contain all those items that make up your Family Management Plan.

The key is never forget that everything you are writing down is relationally motivated – it's rooted in love, and designed to foster harmony among everyone involved. These tools should be bathed in careful thought and executed with a heavy dose of grace (for your children, your spouse, and especially yourself). You will be amazed at how this process actually transforms your everyday behavior – simply stopping long enough to ask yourself enough questions, having a goal in mind, parenting on purpose, rather than out of survival or crisis aversion. This planning process and the resulting plans will equip you with the tools, knowledge, and skills to help you effectively fulfill your parenting roles.

7

HOW TO DEVELOP A FAMILY GOAL STATEMENT

Perhaps the most helpful thing my wife and I did as parents was to develop Family Goals. Because we used the goals as a starting point for creating rules and consequences, referring to our goals helped us maintain perspective as we navigated the difficult and challenging experiences we had when our kids were tweens and teens. They were our "30,000 ft. view" of what we were trying to accomplish, and the standards against which we could check ourselves as we made difficult, gut-wrenching decisions like sending one of our children away to a wilderness camp and/or whether we should bail the same child out of jail for the second time in a year.

Family Goals are brief statements that specify the values, beliefs, attitudes, character traits, and behaviors you want your family and children to adopt and maintain. These goals should be future-oriented and challenging, but also specific, motivating, and achievable.

Sitting down to brainstorm about these goals shouldn't be an arduous process – it should be done with a proper reverence for the seriousness of the task – but shouldn't neglect humor and fun, either! You're trying to foster genuine, loving bonds between human beings and motivate your children to see the value in responsibility and character-building, not trying to increase the bottom line of a Fortune 500 company.

Each family goal is held up as a worthy ideal family members are encouraged to work together to achieve and sustain. These ideals will become a sort of measuring stick through which you can evaluate how well you are doing, both as a family, and as individuals within the family. But more than anything, they're reminders of the people you want to be together and individually. A strong goal will paint a picture of a family any healthy person wants to be in.

The goals you make can all be combined into a single Family Goal Statement (FGS). You may want to call it Organized Chaos or Perfectly Imperfect – if you've got creative blood in the family, take these concepts and make them your own. A good FGS should list and briefly describe each important goal, and some activities family members will engage in to achieve this goal.

When you create your FGS, it is important all family members have ownership and the opportunity to participate in offering suggestions about each goal and what they can do to help achieve it. This is called 'buy-in'. For example, if one of your family goals is for each family member to be happy, some viable suggestions are, "We will always try to be kind," or "Let's treat each other the way we want to be treated." An important principle to keep in mind here is the entire family should have input on each family goal.

I cannot emphasize enough the need for the tweens' and teens' participation in this process – parents should have been preparing thoughtfully for the conversation, but it should not be presented as information to be received and digested without seeking some input on the front end. Teens desperately need to know their input is welcome and valued, not forgotten or placated.

When we included our children in the process of goal setting, we would say something like, "Hey, we want to talk to you about some family goals. As parents, we are supposed to help you become healthy, happy adults who are successful at navigating all kinds of challenges. Your mom and I have talked about this a lot and decided to set some family goals." We then explained what family goals are, and we always tried to make the process fun and collaborative.

Once you have formulated your FGS, it should be displayed in a prominent place in your home to remind each family member of the ideals represented by the Statement. If someone in the family is artistic, give them the opportunity to design the physical appearance of the statement and allow it to become a part of the general décor rather than looking like a framed contract on the wall.

A sample FGS is provided here. Use this example to guide you in developing your own FGS. First, list the values, beliefs, attitudes, character traits, and behaviors you want your family and children to work toward adopting and maintaining. For example, you may want your family members to be 1) happy, 2) fun-loving, 3) safe, 4) healthy, 5) talented, 6) humble, 7) modest, 8) respectful, 9) frugal, 10) environmentally sensitive, 11) orderly, 12) law-abiding, 13) moral, 14) ethical, 15) productive, 16) independent, 17) honest, 18) service-oriented, 19) socially adept, 20) trustworthy, 21) courageous, 22) responsible, 23) patient, 24) persistent, 25) self-confident, 26) assertive, 27) flexible, 28) competent, 29) forgiving, 30) hard working, and/or 31) spiritually balanced.

On the other hand, if you are not so comprehensive (or anal retentive), you could limit yourself to maybe 8 or 10 of these items, to simplify your life.

An alternate list might include happy, safe, healthy, respectful, ethical, productive, honest, and self-confident. In your situation, you might say, "Hey, if we could accomplish this much as a family, I would consider it a whopping success!" And you would be 100% right!

In either case, and yes, you can make a case for approaching it either way, but do listen to your kids, who will tell you that, in this project, less is better, less is simpler, and less just might get their initial buy in.

Then, list and briefly describe, each of these goals in Column 1 of the worksheet. After listing your goals, ask family members to offer suggestions on what they are willing to do, individually and collectively, to help achieve each goal. List these suggestions in column 2 of the worksheet.

Sample Family Goal Statement	
Family Goal	What will family members do to help achieve the goal?
Our family members will be safe.	We will not give our names or address to strangers on the Internet. We will wear seatbelts every time we ride in an automobile.
Our family will work toward and cooperate in keeping our house and yard in order.	We will do all our assigned chores in a timely manner.
Our family will be supportive of other family members.	When possible, we will attend the activities of other family members, such as concerts, soccer games, plays, and award ceremonies. We will give encouragement to other family members when they are trying to overcome problems.
Our family will communicate in ways that strengthen family relationships.	We will learn to avoid using "bad conversation habits" like name-calling. We will listen to and validate the opinions and feelings of other family members.

Once again, whenever possible, look for opportunities to have fun with this process. If your children have creative personalities, give them some leeway to pepper in whatever makes them laugh, as long as it somewhat represents a good character trait. Some irreverence can go a long way with teens, and "inside jokes" strengthen bonds. If your goal is to be respectful and they want to say, "We will never leave the toilet seat up" or "We will commit to telling one another if one of us has something in our teeth in public."

As your kids make these goals their own, they're being encouraged to join a story that's greater than their own, and beginning to visualize the responsibility they have for others. I wonder if I could count how many times I've heard in my counseling practice these five words: "I never thought of that!" Well, in setting goals together as a family, no one has that excuse any longer. Our current consumeristic culture preaches a loud message to our young people that their greatest measure of truth should be their feelings, but anyone who's lived a little can tell you that won't get you very far when it comes to paying a mortgage or staying in a committed relationship when things get hard. This goal-setting process helps them begin to see how they can contribute to a greater whole instead of focusing on what the world (or, in this case, you as the parent) is willing to indulge them in.

Once you have developed and prominently displayed the goals outlined in your FGS, you should refer to them often.

To encourage our children to adopt the goals listed on our FGS, my wife and I typically set aside time in our weekly family meeting (to be introduced shortly) to discuss a particular goal. For example, one of the goals included in our FGS is to "show support for other family members." When discussing this goal during one of our family meetings, my wife and I explained to our children we would like them to show support for their siblings by attending their athletic events, plays, and other activities. We further reinforced this expectation by setting aside time in our weekly family meeting to discuss the upcoming activities of each family member and, in turn, encouraging all family members to attend. This type of advance notice provides our older children, who have many activities of their own, the opportunity to plan to attend their siblings' activities.

Before embarking on managing your children, you need to begin (or continue, whichever the case), a process of bringing *your* attitudes and actions in line with the goals outlined in your goal statement. I'll repeat the old adage as many times as it takes – "Children will follow your example, not your advice." What your children observe in your behavioral patterns is what you will more than likely observe in their attitudes and actions when they become adults. Children have the unique ability to see past our words and focus on our attitudes and behaviors. Although there are no perfect parents, the more closely you align your behaviors with your FGS, the more likely it is you will be able to authentically guide and influence your children to do the same.

8

THE PLANNING AND ORGANIZING GUIDE

It is important to systematically plan the activities you will use to achieve your family goals. Some of the most important reasons for conscientiously planning and organizing your family affairs are to

1) set directions,
2) identify resources you need to get where you want to go,
3) examine alternative courses of action, and
4) develop an action plan with specific assignments.

If you follow the process I recommend, you will plan who will do what, when, where, and how often *before* the activity happens.

Before beginning the planning process, decide what aspects of your family life you want to plan. In my experience, a great place to start is to create plans for things like 1) a weekly family meeting, 2) maintaining the household, 3) work, 4) meal preparation, 5) finances, 6) education, 7) recreation, 8) communication, 9) conflict resolution, and 10) personal development.

Again, this list might be too far reaching for your situation. A bare bones approach might only include a weekly family meeting, maintaining the household, finances, education, and conflict resolution (could be included in the family meeting).

The bottom line when considering what to plan is simple: Whatever aspects of your family life you hope to organize and manage efficiently should be carefully and thoughtfully planned.

The tool I recommend for planning is called the Planning and Organizing Guide (POG). My wife and I used this process to remind ourselves we need to be clear when we are giving guidance to our kids. We also wanted to spell out why we wanted things done a certain way, what was in it for the kids, and how they could do what we wanted them to do in a way that met our approval. Throughout the process, we encouraged input and creativity. In fact, many of our best ideas came from our children. And, as you can imagine, when the children provided input that shaped anything they were involved in, (buy-in in its simplest form) they were more likely to be excited about participating in the conversation.

Note there is ANOTHER sample POG plan in the Appendix.

| **Planning and Organizing Guide (POG)** |||||

1. List all the things you want to plan. For example, household maintenance, recreation, education. Each of these items will become a separate section in your Plan.
2. Complete a separate POG form for each of the items listed. Don't hesitate to modify this form and create your own, for you may have an approach that works better for your specific circumstances. The important thing is to systematically plan and *follow through*.
   A. Write the item you want to plan in row 1.
   B. In column 1, list all those things you want to plan under the area you are focused on at this time.
   C. In column 2, describe what you want done in connection with each item in column 1.
   D. In column 3, describe who will do how much of what, how often, by when, and where to accomplish what you want done.
   E. In column 4, record when and how you will follow up to determine if the specific actions items in column 3 have been accomplished.
   F. Record special instructions in the bottom row of the chart.

Area of Focus:

List Things You Want To Plan under this Area	Describe What You Want Done	Describe Who Will Do How Much of What, by When, and Where	Record When and How You Will Follow Up on Action Items

Planning and Organizing Guide (POG)			
Monthly Family Activity	Present ideas for family activity to family members at weekly family meeting. After activity has been selected, determine what needs to be done to plan the activity and make assignments to appropriate family members.	Dad will present four different options for a family activity to all family members at the next family meeting. Family members will select an option and Dad will make assignments, as he deems appropriate. Dad will follow up to determine whether assignments are accomplished and make family members aware of what they need to do to prepare for the activity.	Dad will follow up at each of the next four family meetings (more often, if necessary) to determine whether assignments have been made and to inform family members of what they need to do to prepare for the activity.
Special instructions:			

Special instructions:

I suggest that a specific time be set aside for developing your family plans. It is ideal to retreat to a place where you can focus your attention on developing and refining the plan. The plan should *always* be considered a work in progress because you will need to modify it as circumstances change and as you gain experience in raising your children. No one should expect to have it down right out of the gate!

Shortly after the plan is initially developed, and every time it is modified, you should seek feedback on the plan before it is fully implemented. Most importantly, you should seek your children's input before the plan is finalized. Let your children know you value their comments unless, of course, they are expressed in a disrespectful manner. Allow your children to express themselves openly, even on items you have already internally determined as non-negotiable items. Record their suggestions and feedback to demonstrate you are taking them seriously.

Once you have received feedback on the plan, meet again with your spouse or parenting partner (if you have one) and consider how to use the feedback to improve the plan. After the plan has been revised, call a meeting with your children, and go over the plan you're proposing. Let the children know when you intend to implement the plan. Also, let them know that the plan is a living document that will be revisited on a regularly scheduled

basis (i.e., every four to six months). Schedule the next time you will talk about the plan as a family. Each time you ask for input on the plan, record the comments and meet in private with your spouse to use the feedback you get to improve the plan.

A note on framing this conversation for your children.

In all things, don't neglect to review the *why*. If putting together this plan feels like a homework assignment to you, then it will feel like a homework assignment to your children. If you present it in an unfeeling, matter-of-fact way, you're increasing the chances your tweens and teens will resent the process and rebel against it. Our "why" always comes back to the values we want to instill in our kids – not just teaching them the right things to do "just because," but taking the time to explain *why* certain actions in life are likely to cause you to lose important relationships, get fired from your job, or communicate poorly with others.

Do not change the plan in the presence of your children. Always retreat with your spouse or parenting partner when you are thinking about changing something. If you don't, you run the risk of the children manipulating the plan by playing you against your spouse or by appealing to your emotions at a time when they want something very badly that goes against your better judgment and the agreed upon plan. We all think we're too smart to get played, but then it sneaks up on us before we realize it!

Place the plan in a colorful binder in a location where everyone in the family has ready access to it.

Organizing naturally follows planning. After you've figured out what you want to do and what you'll need in order to do it, you organize it in a way that will make it successful. This involves making sure you and your children have ready access to all the information, resources, equipment, outside services, and so on, required to implement and achieve your goals. For example, if you want your children to perform specific chores, you should make sure they have ready access to the tools they need to carry out their assigned responsibilities. If you expect them to study for one hour every day, you should provide a place in your home where they can study without being disturbed. Column 3 in the POG (decide who will do how much, of what, by when, where, and how often) is designed to help you organize the family goals you have planned to accomplish.

Don't forget to plan for the unexpected. Be flexible, and where it is appropriate, build in contingency plans. For example, what happens when the child who is responsible for doing the dishes is sick? Are the dishes left undone? Is the child required to do the dishes on an assigned night if he or she has a highly communicable disease? Obviously, there needs to be some back-up plans to cover contingencies. These contingency plans should be recorded under the action section of your Family Management Plan.

Admittedly, formulating a Family Management Plan is no easy task. It requires a significant investment of time, and, when two parents are involved, it can become a real struggle that requires a fair bit of negotiation. You may find yourself wondering if you've signed yourself up for more headache than you started with. However, an important side benefit comes from the planning process itself. This process, more often than not, requires considerable self-disclosure, negotiation, and compromise. If you and your spouse or parenting partner approach this process seriously, by investing the time and energy required to "put your ducks in a row" (out of earshot of your children), your family management (parenting) efforts will become more and more refined, effective, and efficient over time.

9
SETTING AND JUSTIFYING FAMILY RULES

ALL FAMILIES HAVE RULES, WRITTEN AND UNWRITTEN. WHETHER they're developed and enforced by parents, written out and framed, or simply just "understood" because of a particular family member's emotional hold on others – you're already operating on some kind of rule system. The key to a healthy family structure is to be *intentional* about how those rules are developed and *clear* about how they're communicated. A family's rules should be rooted in the family's values. When possible, they should anticipate rather than react. What I mean is this: there will be times new family rules will be developed as a result of poor choices shown by members of the family. But, whenever possible, these rules should be created to foster the family environment you're looking to create, rather than mitigating damage.

Family rules help the family achieve family goals by 1) mandating behaviors that contribute to the goals, and by 2) prohibiting behaviors that may prevent the goals from being achieved. For example, if a family goal is to do well in school, a family rule designed to support this goal might state, "All students in the family will complete all homework assignments before watching television."

One way parents can successfully set the stage for family rules is by presenting rules that impact *everyone's* behavior, not just the children. By doing so, children learn there is a greater purpose behind the rules than listening to you "just because". "Because I said so," is not a *wrong* thing to say to a child, but there are certainly *more effective* ways to communicate and teach them the larger values behind right behavior. This doesn't mean everyone in the family is subjected to the same rules, but it does mean all individuals can be held accountable for their own behavior. Modeling a proper response when one of your children catches you breaking a rule can be a powerful tool for relationship-building. It demonstrates mutual respect and reminds your children you care about how *you* behave also, not just how they behave.

Rules can also contribute to family chores/projects and activities by setting a framework for who will engage in each activity and how, when, where, and how often such activities are to be performed. For example, a rule about doing the dishes might state, "On Monday, Wednesday, and Friday evening, Jordan will rinse and place all dinner dishes in the dishwasher before 9 p.m."

You should link all family rules to family goals and activities. This will help you justify the rule and ensure all rules contribute to your efforts to establish and maintain a healthy, functional family.

My wife and I have established many rules over the years. Some of our rules are as follows:

- You will do all your assigned chores in a timely manner.
- You will not use the property of others without first getting their permission.
- You will attend all family meetings (unless you have been excused in advance).
- You will show support for family members by attending their activities (when possible).

SETTING AND JUSTIFYING FAMILY RULES

- You will not use vulgar or profane words.
- You will always tell the truth.
- You will do your homework before you watch television or play video games.
- You will apologize and make amends for personal mistakes that impact others.
- You will resolve conflicts peacefully, without raising your voice or hitting/pushing/grabbing the other person.
- While living at home, you will attend Church/Synagogue/Mosque every week, unless you have a good reason not to.
- You will not stay out past your curfew.
- Before leaving the house, you will always let your parents know where you plan to go, what you plan to do, and when you plan to be home.
- You will treat your family and friends with kindness and respect.
- When we have trouble communicating, we will use structured communication. (Structured communication is described in a later chapter.)

The Family Rule Development Guide (Table 1) that follows will guide you through the process of setting, justifying, and deciding on consequences for all family rules. Writing these things down can be a great tool for working through them! First, list all rules in column 1. Now, when starting out, let me recommend, as an alternative to listing 15 or 20 or more rules, start with the most important 5 or 8 or even 10 at most. It will be much easier to keep track, get on track, get the family's cooperation and buy-in, and stay on track with this. In column 2, provide a justification for each rule listed in the first column. Typically, the justification should explain how the rule helps to 1) achieve one or more family goals and/or 2) ensure one or more family activities are carried out as planned. Again, no lengthy explanations. A line or two at most makes the point. There is no need for deep explanations on this chart. In column 3, you will list consequences for not abiding by a family rule. (Table 3a in the Appendix will also help with this part.)

As a reminder, your family goals are based on the story you're writing together: who do you want to be as a family? As individuals? Your family rules should be based on these important, identity-seeking questions. Think into the future. Your children do not only need to learn to relate to the other people in their household and keep a general sense of peace, but they also need to learn how to relate with others outside the home. Make sure you remember, and remind your children, these rules are designed to daily remind *everyone* of your strong foundation as human beings, good citizens, etc.

SETTING AND JUSTIFYING FAMILY RULES 39

Table 1. The Family Rule Development Guide			
Family Rule Must support at least one family goal.	**Justification for Rule** Consider benefits of rule and how it supports goals/activities.	**Consequence(s)** Apply discipline via natural or logical consequences.

When setting rules, you want to identify some basic core rules and then support these core rules by establishing several small preventive rules. Here is a great example of starting broadly, and as your family adapts to using this guide, then adding more detailed and subcategory rules. For example: If you have a core rule stating, "Don't use drugs," then once the dust settles, you will want to add some preventive rules such as **WHO** your teen may associate with, **WHAT** types of activities are allowed, **WHERE** your teen is allowed to go, and **WHEN** your teen may go–as well as **WHEN** he or she is expected to return.

It would be foolish to believe your teen could hang out at the wrong places or associate with drug-using friends and remain drug-free. When you create preventive rules alongside your main core rules, you provide your teen with the greatest amount of protection. You also become involved, so you can be aware of problems early and resolve them before they become overwhelming.

Try to have helpful, proactive conversations about these things as a family rather than lecturing about them in reaction to bad behavior. The more you can anticipate, the more you will be set up for success in the long run. You will see in the Sample Rule Development Guide in the Appendix, the consequences for breaking a rule is not always necessarily disciplinary or from the "top-down," but they do describe the logical end toward making a particular choice. An example is this: the first rule we have is about our commitment to using structured communication. You will see the consequence of not using structured communication is not really a disciplinary action, so much as it is simply a result. If you choose to communicate poorly (or not at all), you will probably experience more frustration and difficulty in your relationships. This is an important lesson for your children to learn. (Not to mention an important reminder for any of us, no matter what stage of life we're in!)

The best practice I can recommend is to work through a draft of these rules with your spouse or parenting partner. Once the most important, basic rules have been established in draft form, you may want to share them with your children for feedback. This increases the ownership the children will have over how they are agreeing to behave. After receiving feedback, revise your rules accordingly and produce a final set of rules, justifications, and consequences. Share this final set of rules with your children and let them know the rules will be upheld until further notice. Revisit the rules on a periodic basis to revise, if necessary, those rules that are flawed (e.g., impractical, unenforceable, too lenient, not specific).

If you are implementing this process while one or more of your children are not in a place to contribute productively to this conversation, be patient. Make sure your expectations of your children is realistic. Do your best to give them every opportunity to share while you actively listen. Don't expect to knock it out of the park at your first family meeting. These things take time and practice, and you may have a teen who is wholly resistant to the conversation from the outset, but later, once you have demonstrated your own accountability to the family rules, may open up.

10

HOW TO ENFORCE FAMILY RULES

When children willfully violate family rules and are resistant to counsel, it will be necessary to enact the previously set consequence/s. The process of carrying out consequences in response to misbehavior is called discipline. Discipline is a form of teaching and correcting that is designed to help all family members live within the agreed-upon set of rules. Discipline should not be confused with punishment, and it is important both parents and children understand that. It is designed to help remind everyone what happens when we value our own will above the common good.

Discipline is a contingency relationship: when a rule is broken, a consequence either happens naturally or is instituted by a parent. The underlying principle is based on the assumption an undesired behavior will decrease if followed by an unpleasant consequence. As a matter of practice, I have often talked to my children about my role in disciplining them. I recommend you do the same. Explain what you are trying to do by disciplining them: "Our society expects me, as your parent, to socialize you in a way that helps you understand there are consequences for breaking rules and laws. If I (your loving parent) don't teach this principle to you, someone who does not love you, will!"

There are number of go-to disciplinary options that can be administered to get your child's attention and hopefully redirect their actions. These include:

1. "Grounding" or restricting movement (such as in a time-out)
2. Removing privileges (such as having friends over or using the phone)
3. Restricting the use of personal items or removing them altogether (such as favorite clothes or stereo)
4. Verbal correction
5. Extra service hours

The primary concern when selecting a consequence is to identify those consequences that produce the degree of unpleasantness required to cause the child to stop misbehaving.

Some general thoughts to keep in mind as you approach the discipline process:

- The "level" of discipline should be proportional to the offense. When discipline is out of proportion to the infraction, and/or when it is administered harshly, it can do more harm than good. I am also convinced insufficient discipline can result in negative consequences – you will not do your child any favors by turning a blind eye to the same repeated negative behaviors.
- The punishment should fit the crime – and the child.
- The discipline should always be carried out in appropriate, loving ways.
- The secret is balance and patience. Neither is likely to prevail, however, unless you have planned ahead about how the discipline will look, in what instances it will be

implemented, who will administer it, how, how often, how intensely, etc.

There are two broad categories of consequences that allow a young person to experience the actual result of his or her own behavior. I have labeled these natural and logical consequences.

Natural consequences are the direct result of a person's behavior. Examples include getting injured when jumping off a high ledge, getting bitten when petting an unfamiliar dog, or getting arrested for driving over the speed limit.

Logical consequences are established by the parents and are the direct and logical consequence of the transgression; consequences should not be arbitrarily imposed. Examples include losing the privilege to use the family car after getting a speeding ticket, being restricted from using the computer after visiting pornography sites, having to pay for a broken window after hitting a ball into the window, or receiving extra chores after not completing regularly assigned tasks.

What follows is a list of natural and logical consequences for use when dealing with noncompliance with family rules. These consequences are not in any particular order and should be applied with justice in mind. As the saying goes, "The punishment should always fit the crime."

Grounding: I start with grounding is because in my experience as a therapist, it is one of the most popular tactics used by parents. In my opinion, it is also the most *misused* tool in the toolbox because it often comes from a parent's mouth as a spontaneous response to any number of different misbehaviors. Parents also often apply this consequence without thinking through the implications grounding has on *them*. This is why parents often modify grounding after tempers cool. And, when it is modified, the children learn the worst possible lesson from their parents— their parents are not consistent and discipline is not predictable.

I do believe grounding is a great tool if it is used correctly and in the context of a thought-out parenting plan. So, how is grounding carried out correctly?

First, you must realize when you ground a child, you are actually grounding yourself! If you really mean your child is going to stay home all weekend and not do anything except sit on his or her bed and contemplate misbehavior, a responsible adult will need to stay home and observe the punishment as it takes place.

A much better approach is to assign chores or responsibilities to the child who is on restriction. And, once the extra chores are assigned, explain to the child the restriction is not over until all the chores are completed. This approach has many advantages:

1. The family benefits from the work that is getting done by the child/teen on restriction.
2. It is easy to monitor and observe the beginning and end of the restriction.
3. It allows the offender to control how long he or she is on restriction. It is also good practice for "unruly children" who, later on, may experience community service by court order.

Having to do extra work is much more reflective of what happens in life when you make a typical poor choice, whereas grounding represents what happens when you make a detrimentally poor choice (you go to jail).

Once again, grounding and all the disciplinary measures that follow, should be carried out with love, in an even temper, and within the guidelines of your parenting plan. This way you and your child know the rules and the consequences that follow noncompliance.

11

THE FAMILY SERVICE DISCIPLINE APPROACH

THE DISCIPLINE TECHNIQUE OUR FAMILY USES WAS INSPIRED BY BENIGN version of the "community service" dealt to some of my clients who broke the law. We call it the Family Service Discipline Program or the FSDP. Just like court-ordered community service, it helps get some work done in the community (the family in this case), and teaches errant community members (the unruly tweens and teens in the household) to fall in line with community laws and family rules.

As with any form of discipline, implementing and managing this program requires time and effort. However, our experience has been the return on this investment far outweighs the cost. And, when carried out in conjunction with a parenting plan, this disciplinary tactic reinforces family goals and rules in a powerful and effective way. It also helps parents calibrate discipline in a more fair and consistent way that is aligned with the idea that "the punishment should fit the crime."

To set up a Family Service Discipline Program (FSDP) you must do the following:

1. Make or purchase something that can represent a Family

Service Token (FST). We used poker chips.
2. Write a number on each chip and place them in a non-transparent container. This number will correspond to a chore on your Family Service Chore Chart (FSCC).
3. List all of your family rules (and goals if you like) in the second column of a three-column matrix (see Table 2a below). Number each rule consecutively in column 1. In column three of this matrix, assign a number of FSTs. Assign a higher number of FSTs to very serious rules, and a lower number of FSTs to less serious rules. Just as those who commit armed robbery in a community are more severely punished than a person who drives 10 miles over the speed limit, so your children should pay a steeper price when they break a rule like "you may not take the car without permission," as compared to "you must make your bed before you go to school in the morning."
4. Develop a Family Service Chore Chart or FSCC (see Table 2). This is a list of separate chores your children can do in about the same amount of time. For example, wash the dishes, vacuum the upstairs, vacuum the downstairs, clean an upstairs bathroom, sweep the garage, rake the backyard, rake the front yard, organize the garage, clean out and organize the pantry, pick up all the toys in the playroom, and so on. If you have both tweens and teenagers you will need to develop at least two different age-appropriate lists.
5. Write instructions for the FSDP. Place these instructions in the front of a notebook that contains the Family Service Chore Chart. These instructions should say something like this:

The purpose of the FSDP is to enforce and help teach you the importance of our family rules. These rules are included in this notebook. Alongside each rule is a number of FSTs. Each FST has a number on it which is

THE FAMILY SERVICE DISCIPLINE APPROACH   47

assigned to a specific rule. If you break a rule, you will be asked to reach into the FST container and select the number of FSTs assigned to that particular rule. For example, if you don't do your homework on time, you will be given 2 FSTs. This means you must do the two chores listed on the Family Service Chore Chart (Table 2b) that correspond with the numbers on the FSTs you pick from the FST container. You will be restricted from watching television and getting on the computer and talking to your friends on the phone and going outside and doing anything else you may enjoy until you have completed the two chores on the Family Service Chore Chart that correspond to the numbers on the two FSTs you picked from the FST container.

Introduce the FSDP to your children. Explain in clear detail how it will work. Tell them you will test this program for a period of time (a week or two), make a few changes, and then implement the program in earnest.

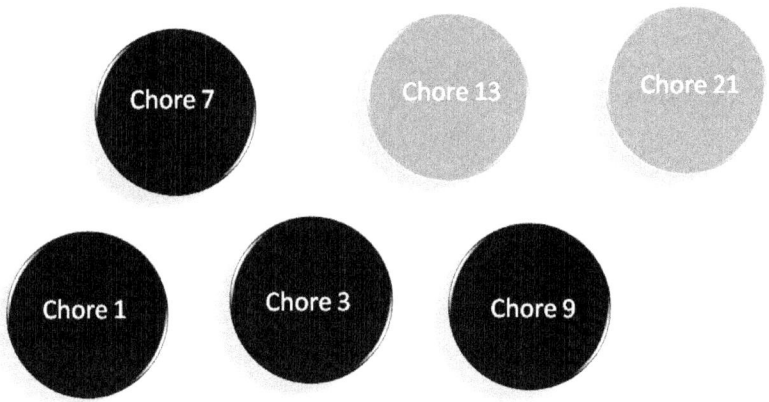

	Table 2a Family Rules Chart	
Rule Number	The Name of the Rule	Number of FSTs Assigned to Rule
1	You must not hit your brother or sister	5
2	You must make your bed before you go to school	1
3	No TV or iPad until your homework is done	2
4	You must not speak disrespectfully to your parents	2
5	You may not use something that does not belong to you without asking and getting permission	3

Notes and Alternatives:

- If the offense committed had a direct effect on another person and it makes sense (e.g. you hit another person or use their things without permission), a chore could be selected by a parent that has a direct benefit to the offended party (such as taking over one of their chores).
- Write "Pass" on a few of the tokens. This is a fun variation, but is also consistent with the real world –

there are times that we do things we shouldn't and there aren't consequences, but we should never count on that.
- Instead of chores, write acts of service that cause the child to think outside their own selfishness. Examples could include choosing a small gift for a family member, visiting an elderly relative and/or writing them a card, or giving time to a community organization.
- Give the child an opportunity to "pick their poison" before having to pull a token out of the jar. If they can come up with activities that care for the family, aren't listed on tokens, and you find them acceptable, reward their ingenuity by letting them design their own consequence.

Table 2b: The Family Service Chore Chart

Table 2b. The Family Service Chore Chart		
Chore Number	The Name of the Chore	How The Chore Must Be Done
1	Dinner Dishes	
2	Vacuum Upstairs	
3	Clean Upstairs Bathroom	
4	Sweep the Garage	
5	Serve the Family at Dinner	
6	Wash the Family Car	
7	Do the Week's Meal Planning	
8	Clean Up Dog Poop	
9	Do Family's Laundry	
10	Pull Weeds	

Apology: Apologies are one way individuals repair damaged relationships. The child/teen may be asked to apologize to the offended party (e.g., parent or sibling) in writing or in person. It is important that the offending child/teen accept blame for the incident and demonstrate authentic regret when offering the apology, or nothing will have been accomplished.

Behavioral Contract: The child/teen and parent work out a written agreement that outlines specific positive behaviors the child/teen is to engage in (or specific negative behaviors he or she is to avoid), the privileges or rewards the child/teen will earn for complying with the behavioral contract, and the terms by which the child/teen is to earn the rewards (e.g., making his or her bed for three consecutive days). Likewise, the consequences of not complying with the specific requirements outlined in the contract should be recorded in the contract. Invite your tween or teen to be a part of developing the contract terms as they think through why the behavior change is important. As might be noted here, this does NOT have to be a formal contract… a few lines on a piece of paper agreed to by parent and child is sufficient.

Community service – with friends. If your child gets in trouble with their friends, consider a way you could have your child invite those same friends into a positive behavior. Maybe you volunteer to serve at a homeless shelter and have your teen invite one of those friends to participate with you, or have those friends over for a family dinner rather than just hanging out with peers.

12

ADDITIONAL AND ALTERNATIVE DISCIPLINES

Discipline choices: Give your child a chance to "pick their poison." Would they rather pay money, do chores around the house, listen to a lecture, or set aside a privilege? Ask them how they believe they should make it right. This gives them an opportunity to reflect on what they did and take ownership of the next steps rather than just having to react to what you present to them.

Learning Opportunity: Engage the child in a life lesson that has to do with their misbehavior. If a child's irresponsibility has a financial impact, such as breaking or losing an item, have them complete a short math comparison of the cost of the item and how many hours of work would be involved to replace it, so they understand the impact of having to replace things. If your child doesn't have an allowance, have them determine how the item can be paid for by sacrificing things you would regularly buy for them.

Make the world a better place: If your tween or teen has demonstrated negative social behavior, in addition to having them repair the relationship they damaged, ask what they might do that cares for their community and/or strengthens other relationships. This gives them an opportunity to think about how people "should" behave in the world and how they can go out of their way to practice it.

Money Talks: Think through different ways to financially reward your child in ways that reflect how money and success work in the real world. Consider having them pay for things they have failed to complete, whether that's homework, housework, or other responsibilities. Conversely, consider rewarding your child for pro-success activities. An act of boldness (trying out a new sport, hobby, or skill that you know intimidates the child) could be financially rewarded. Taking risks in life can both costs us and rewards us. Think creatively about how these concepts might translate into paying and/or "charging" your child for their actions. Rather than actually asking your child to give you money, a pot of money can be set aside that is contributed to and withdrawn from at different times according to their decisions.

Over-correction: The child/teen is required to repetitively practice a skill that will "replace" or improve upon an inappropriate or problematic behavior. For example, a child/teen who does several other things before carrying out a parent's request to go to his room and do his homework may have to stay in after school one day and take several "practice" trips to his room, where he gets out his books, reviews his assignments, and begins doing his homework. In this example, the parent might accompany the child/teen to monitor how promptly he walks to his room and to give the child/teen feedback about how much the target behavior has improved. Another example of over-correction is to assign additional chores to a child/teen who has neglected assigned chores.

Verbal Correction: In the typical reprimand, the parent approaches the child/teen, states the child/teen is misbehaving, and instructs the child/teen to stop misbehaving immediately. Reprimands should refer to the undesirable behavior and not slander the child's character. They should be kept short to avoid arguments with the child/teen. Do your best to gather yourself beforehand– remember, your disappointment does not need to be communicated under high emotion. If you are confident in the form of discipline you have chosen for this infraction, trust the natural process. The volume of your voice is not going to make your discipline more effective, especially with a teen.

Reprimands should be used sparingly, as child/teen may become defiant if repeatedly confronted by an angry parent. If used too frequently and indiscriminately, verbal reprimands lose their effectiveness and become reinforcers of undesired behavior because they grant attention to the child. Verbal reprimands given by parents during time-outs are a major cause of reduced effectiveness of this form of discipline.

Redirection: The parent interrupts problem behavior by calling on the child/teen to answer a question, assigning him or her a task to carry out, or otherwise refocusing the child's attention. This demonstrates to the child they are not going to achieve their desired result by the way they have chosen to behave.

Reasoning, or Away-from-the-Moment Discussions: In general, it is more effective to anticipate and prevent misbehavior than to punish it. "Away from the moment" refers to dealing with difficult behavior not in the heat of the moment, but instead, in advance, or away from the actual misbehavior. An away-from-the-moment discussion provides the parent with opportunities to teach what behavior is acceptable. It has the potential to serve as a very useful tool to prevent undesirable behavior, because it allows the parent to teach the child/teen the desirable behavior in anticipation. For example, if you child/teen misbehaves in a public setting, you can choose to address your concern in a private setting at home instead of making a scene at the site of the infraction.

Positive Communication Rehearsal: When individuals are having difficulty communicating or are not willing to communicate in healthy ways (i.e., they have one or more conversational bad habits such as blaming or eye-rolling), they can be required to practice positive communication using a structured communication method. The rules are as follows:

1. One person speaks at a time. This person is designated as the speaker. This person expresses thoughts, concerns, and desires in a respectful manner to another person who is designated as the listener.
2. The listener is encouraged to become curious about what the speaker is saying by listening carefully to what is being said and, after the speaker has spoken, simply paraphrases what the speaker has said. That is, the listener repeats back, in his or her own words, what the speaker said as a way to demonstrate to the speaker that he or she is listening. A simple format that can be followed by the listener is—

What I heard you say is (paraphrase what the sender said) .

Is that right?
Is there more?

1. After the speaker feels like the receiver understands what he or she has to say, the roles reverse. That is, the speaker becomes the listener, and the listener begins to speak.

NOTE: *to make this back and forth communication more fun we have a microphone we give to the designated "speaker." The rule then is no one gets to speak (other than asking questions for clarification and paraphrasing what they hear) unless they are holding the microphone. This can become quite funny as we watch everyone who is in the conversation (the designated listeners) asking for the microphone instead of listening. It's also very instructive in that my wife and I can more readily point out the role of speaker vs listener.*

Promise: The parent approaches the misbehaving child/teen and informs that he or she has behaved inappropriately. The parent asks the child/teen to state an appropriate alternative behavior he or she should have followed. The parent then requests the child/teen promise the parent (verbally or in writing) he or she will not engage in this misbehavior again.

Reflective Essay: The child/teen is required to write and submit to the parent a brief composition after displaying ill behavior. At minimum, the composition would state (1) what problem behavior the child/teen displayed, (2) how the child/teen could have acted in an alternative, more acceptable manner, and (3) a promise from the child/teen to show appropriate behaviors in similar situations in the future.

*Note: Some parents use a pre-printed, structured questionnaire containing these three items for the child/teen to complete.

Response Cost: Usually, response cost programs first award a child/teen a certain number of tokens with no conditions attached. Throughout the monitoring period, the child/teen has a token withdrawn whenever he or she displays a behavior that is inappropriate. (These behaviors usually have been agreed upon in advance.) The child/teen is permitted to "cash in" any points he or she still retains at the end of the monitoring period or may be allowed to "bank" the points toward a future reward or privilege.

Restitution: If a child/teen breaks or loses another family member's property, he or she would be required to both apologize for the act and replace the property. If the property is irreplaceable, the child/teen should, at a minimum, pay some compensation for what is lost. The point here is the child/teen engages in an activity that actually or symbolically restores the environment, setting, or social situation his or her misbehavior has damaged.

Rewarding Alternative (Positive) Behaviors: The parent "catches" the child/teen engaging in appropriate behavior and provides positive attention or incentives during these times. The same positive attention or consequences are withheld during times when the child/teen misbehaves.

Rules Review: The parent approaches the misbehaving child/teen and 1) has him or her read off the posted family rules, 2) asks the child/teen which of those rules his or her current behavior is violating, and 3) has the child/teen state what positive behavior he or she will engage in instead.

13

THE USE AND OVERUSE OF 'TIME-OUT"

Time-Out Suspension or Removal of Privileges: For young children, time-out usually involves removing parental attention and praise (ignoring), or placing the child in a chair for a specified time with no adult interaction. For older children and adolescents, this disciplinary measure usually involves removing privileges or denying participation in activities. To be effective, this strategy requires that a valued privilege is removed.

As with grounding, several aspects of time-out must be considered to ensure effectiveness. When time-out is first implemented, it will usually result in increased negative behavior by the child, who will test the new limits with a display of emotional behavior, such as a temper tantrum. This is a normal reaction! When you accept this and don't allow your own emotions to match the child's, you will find your child's outbursts will likely become less frequent.

When time-out is used appropriately, the child's feelings are neither persistent nor damaging to self-esteem, despite the intensity of the reaction. However, if the parent engages in verbal or physical interaction with the child during the time-out, the emotional outburst, as well as the behavior originally targeted, will not only persist, but may in fact worsen. Second, time-out is often not effective immediately, although it is highly effective as a long-term strategy. Third, it is often difficult emotionally for a parent to ignore the child during periods of increased negative behavior or when the child begins pleading and bargaining for time-outs to end. The inability of parents to deal with their own distress during a time-out is one of the most common reasons for its failure. One way to combat this difficulty as you work on your own emotional regulation (it is a process for all of us!) is to rely on your team member: your spouse. If you two are supporting one another well, you can tag-team. One parent can communicate the discipline and the other parent can monitor the discipline is carried out.

Some specific suggestions for effective time-outs include:

- Pick the right place. Be sure the time-out location does not have built-in rewards. The TV should not be on during time-out.
- Time-out should last one minute per year of the child's age, to a maximum of ten minutes. So, this type of time-out begins to lose its effectiveness after about age 8 or 10.
- Prepare the child by helping him or her connect the behavior with the time-out.
- Introduce time-out by 24 months of age.
- Keep time-out quiet. It is not the time for teaching or preaching – save the lesson for later.
- Use time-out for the older child to reflect on his or her misbehavior.
- The parent should be the timekeeper.
- Clear the air afterwards. That is, after time-out is over, it is over, and a new activity can then begin.

Loss of Privileges: The child/teen is informed in advance he or she can access a series of privileges (e.g., use the family car, watch TV, play a video game, spend the night with a friend), if his or her behavior remains appropriate. The parent instructs the child/teen about what kind and intensity of problem behavior may result in the loss of privileges, and for how long. After this introductory phase, the parent withdraws privileges as agreed upon whenever the child/teen misbehaves.

14

PHYSICAL DISCIPLINE AND ANGRY DISCIPLINE

You will find one disciplinary method has been excluded from this list. Over the years, there has been a raging debate among parenting experts regarding whether parents should administer physical discipline. However, this debate has greatly subsided, and it appears the vast majority of experts in this area counsel against physical discipline, noting although hitting a child can have an impact on the child's behavior, in the end, it is simply not effective.

Much of the evidence in this area comes from animal training. Time and again, it has been proven beating animals (as opposed to reinforcing desired behaviors) is simply not effective. Everyone has seen animals carefully nurtured and willing to perform almost any trick for a reward. I have noticed this in the horses I own. The ones trained without beatings are cooperative and sound. The two I have trained the "old-fashioned way," with a whip and intimidation, are distrustful and occasionally dangerous. The point is, beating animals or children, to get them to go along with your will is simply not effective. Hence, when asked my opinion, I encourage parents never hit a tween or teen. Again, after raising five children of our own, my wife and I agree physical discipline should be used with great discretion, if at all.

Without exception, inappropriate and harmful means of discipline include the following: slapping, kicking, punching, arm twisting, shaking, pinching, ear pulling, jabbing, shoving, choking, beating, or delivery of repeated demoralizing blows to the unruly child. These techniques fall outside the range of "disciplinary spanking" and should *never* be implemented.

Another cardinal rule of discipline is worth mentioning here. If at all possible, DO NOT discipline when you are angry. Cool off before setting the terms of discipline. This provides you the time required to get all the facts and consider the motives of the child who committed the infraction. If you ignore this advice, you will more likely than not find yourself overreacting and punishing rather than disciplining. In such cases, it is not uncommon to assign discipline and/or punishment that "does not fit the crime." If you do assign discipline that does not fit the infraction (typically, this happens when we judge out of anger), it is okay to go back to the child and revise the discipline. The more often this occurs, the less responsive your children will be to your parenting overall. Being willing to admit you are wrong is an extremely positive parenting trait likely increase your children's respect for you. Being routinely inconsistent will likely cause their respect to diminish.

To make sure we don't discipline too quickly or from anger, we have told our children any time they break a rule we, as their parents, have 24 hours to make up our mind about the discipline. When you think about it, this is much more similar to how your children will experience discipline as adults. If you violate a traffic law, you typically get a ticket and are required to go to court. This delays the discipline for an extended period of time. If you violate protocol or a policy at work you will likely be asked to talk to supervisor at some point who will privately administer discipline. In other words, we make it a point to wait for up to 24 hours before administering discipline. During this time my wife and I get on the same page about the discipline, why we are administering, and how we will defend our decision (our talking points). Once we've made the decision, we talk to the child privately and explain our decision. After administering the discipline we both tell the child we love them and all this is for their good now and in the future.

Just as being too harsh in your approach to discipline is ineffective and counterproductive, so is being inconsistent and/or too lenient in terms of discipline. Even though parents want to be loved by their children, they should realize from the outset parenting should never be considered a popularity contest. This is particularly true when the two contestants are the parents. Children will, by nature, manipulate any differences of opinion they detect between their parents and will uphold the more lenient parent as the one they "love the most." In other words, children are programmed from birth to play two sides against the middle.

Again, this reinforces the need for parents to delay discipline until they are on the same page about what they plan to do, and for what reason. Parents are a formidable force if they are on the same page about discipline and, especially if they have agreed upon talking points regarding their reasoning and decision. Frankly, as I have helped parents learn this principle I often remind them their children (especially their tweens and teens) are not dogs. They can reason and remember what they did wrong long after the infraction. Hence, as I just mentioned above, delaying discipline is often the better part of wisdom.

It is true a parent can gain the loyalty of one or more of the children by indulging and giving broad license to them. However, this strategy will work against you almost every time. The other spouse or parenting partner, most often, will overcompensate for the lenient parent and may over-discipline. The main result of this disharmony is a stronger allegiance between the child and the more permissive parent, creating a breeding ground for a negative relationship with the "stricter" parent.

Although being the more popular parent has its rewards, it also has its downsides. If you position yourself as the "fun parent," you'll find yourself being constantly being asked permission and subject to pressure tactics designed to get you to give permission. Moreover, the disharmony between the spouses created by the lenience of one partner can have a negative impact on the entire family.

To avoid manipulation and all the other consequences that come with an uneven plan for administering discipline, it is important both parents agree about what the rules are and what disciplines will be administered when the rules have been violated. This requires planning, cooperation, and "buy-in" from both partners.

Another thing to remember when you are assigning discipline is when you punish or restrict your child, you also restrict yourself (and/or your spouse) to the extent you must follow up to make sure your child complies with the discipline. This is why it is so important before either parent administers discipline, both parents discuss the discipline and how it will be carried out. When you discipline without your spouse's consent or "buy in," you can place an undue and unexpected burden on your spouse without proper notice. For example, if your wife is a stay-at-home mom, it may be easy for you to ground your children for a week because all you have to do is pronounce the words while your wife has to literally "stay at home" with them for a week. This is not a problem if your wife agrees to suffer the discipline along with your child. But to arbitrarily assign your wife to policing the home for a week is not fair or considerate.

In summary, to discipline appropriately, you should first be explicit about what you expect of your children and, while remaining calm, hold them accountable when they do not comply. Once again, this technique requires some advanced planning so you and your spouse know what expectations you hold for your children (see the Family Rule Development Guide). It also requires giving yourself time to decide what the best discipline fits the infraction and why.

15

PARTNER/SPOUSAL 'BUY-IN'

WE ADDRESS QUITE A BIT ABOUT PARTNER/SPOUSAL 'BUY-IN', IN MANY situations. While it sounds easy enough, it is often very difficult and not so much because the partners are not in agreement in terms of parenting philosophy or style.

But first, let us address this issue. When two partner/parents are not in sync about parenting, it creates issues between them AND issues with the children. The children figure out right away who is the tough one and the soft one, and manipulate the adults accordingly to their needs. So, even when the parents are not on the same page, they need to agree to some middle ground on each parenting issue for their own sanity.

This is a private, adults only discussion away from the family. Maybe when the kids are in school, at grandparents, or at outside events. You have already seen the most critical issues of parenting laid out in this book, so one by one decide on your joint decision positions on them. Write them out if you have to so there is no argument when the time comes to have to utilize a position.

Once agreed, this is what is called 'buy-in'. You now have a united position with the kids about many, if not all, the issues that come up regularly, and maybe only once in a lifetime, with the kids.

In this way neither of you can be swayed by pleadings from children/teens, nor can you be attacked for a 'nasty' position on some punishment or restriction.

Buy-in may be difficult for other than philosophical reasons. As noted above, if one parent stays home, then grounding means that parent is also grounded for the term of the infraction. That parent may have social, or personal, familial, or even alone time obligations to others or themselves. Now, this schedule is being upset by a partner who has committed the other partner without discussion. It is important to have these discussions ahead of time. As well, plan to use the 24 hour rule indicated above whenever you two aren't sure of a specific punishment, and then get back with the child at hand once you are ready.

The easiest way to engage buy-in with a partner for any reason is to arrange to sit down quietly and discuss a list of situations, incidents, and punishments, handling the resolution to each one and agreeing, or not for each one. Write down the ones agreed to. Write down the disagreements as well and plan to come back to them the next day. Then repeat the process for those that were still in dispute. It won't be long before you have agreement on 90% of the situations, and hopefully, you won't have to deal with the other 10%, or use that 24 hours to iron them out.

16

MOTIVATING AND REWARDING DESIRABLE BEHAVIORS

Without motivation to carry out the Family Management Plan, it's likely family members won't carry out their responsibilities. If this is the case, your best intentions to bring order to the family will remain just that: good intentions. A great plan doesn't mean much if it is not implemented consistently. Implementation comes from motivation, and it's up to the parents to learn how to motivate the family. Of course, it goes without saying the parents must be motivated first and completely and into the program 100%.

Fortunately, researchers have discovered a number of principles that can be applied to increase a child's motivation. The overriding principle I apply in my efforts to motivate my children is called the Premack Principle. This principle is any high probability behavior (things your kids really like to do) can be used to reinforce a low probability behavior (things they do not like to do). I have found this principle has a number of practical advantages that have helped us motivate our children/teenagers to carry out their responsibilities. For example, if I want to motivate our child to do something he or she is not likely to do (a low probability behavior), like sweep the garage or wash the dishes, I must make performing a high probability behavior, like going out with friends, contingent (dependent) upon the low probability. That is, "Yes, you can play video games if you first [the contingency] make your bed and feed the dog."

In psychological literature, the Premack Principle is applied in a motivational learning theory called Operant Conditioning. This theory relies on the principles of contingency, reinforcement, and shaping in the process of motivating compliance with recommended or desired actions.

The principle of contingency suggests that, as is implied by our above example, your child is more likely to carry out his or her responsibilities when the things he or she likes to do are dependent (contingent) upon the performance of a responsibility like mowing the lawn or folding and putting away clothes. (Note how I used this principle of consequences in our Parent/Child Contract). For example: "Son, you may NOT go out with your friends on Friday [a high probability behavior] unless you mow the lawn on Thursday [a low probability behavior]."

On a day-to-day basis, many consequences are contingent upon behavior. For example, getting paid is contingent upon going to work; physical alertness is contingent upon the amount of rest you get; knowledge is dependent upon the amount of training and experience a person has, and so on. The concept of contingency is important here because it is used in connection with reinforcement (or reinforcers) to motivate the performance of assigned duties.

Reinforcement is a principle that refers to the presentation of an event or stimuli which, in turn, results in an increase in the frequency of a desired behavior. There are two types of reinforcement: positive and negative.

A positive reinforcer is distinguished by its specific effect on the desired behavior. If you give your child a reinforcer—like money—in connection with a behavior you want him or her to engage in—like washing the car—and your child's car-washing behavior increases, then the money is a positive reinforcer. Hence, the defining characteristic of a positive reinforcer is its ability to increase the desired behavior it follows, like vacuuming, dusting, homework, taking telephone messages, and so on.

The more common term "reward" is often used synonymously with positive reinforcers. However, in the strictest sense, a reward is not a positive reinforcer unless it actually increases the frequency of a desired behavior. If, for example, you reward your daughter with money for making her bed on Tuesday morning and she chooses not to make her bed on Wednesday morning, the monetary reward was not a positive reinforcer.

Some examples of reinforcers I have used to successfully increase desired behaviors include the following: 1) verbal praise, 2) the privilege of spending the night, 3) money, 4) toys, 5) eating out at a favorite restaurant, 6) ice cream, 7) stickers, 8) check marks on a chore chart, 9) concert tickets, 10) the car, and 11) poker chips that can be cashed in for money.

From the family management perspective, the principle of positive reinforcement carries a strong message: If you can learn to use positive reinforcers, children can be motivated to perform desirable behaviors they wouldn't likely think to do on their own. And the stronger the reinforcer, the more motivation the child will have. Therefore, the very key to motivating our children to carry out their responsibilities lies in our ability to accurately identify strong reinforcers for each child.

Once you have identified your children's individual reinforcers, it becomes possible to use them as a basis for motivating desired performance. Formulating a reinforcement schedule that is designed to apply these principles can help with this process.

A reinforcement schedule can either be continuous or intermittent in nature. Continuous reinforcement requires reinforcing an event every time it occurs. In contrast, intermittent reinforcement requires reinforcing only after your child has done what you want him or her to do a number of times. For example, paying a child five dollars every time he or she washes the car is continuous reinforcement, but paying the child a weekly allowance if (the contingency) he or she completes all assigned chores is an intermittent reinforcer.

In most instances, continuous and intermittent reinforcement schedules produce important differences in the performance of desired behavior. For example, during the initial stages of adopting an assigned behavior, continuous reinforcement is more likely to motivate early performance. For a number of reasons, intermittent reinforcement schedules are preferred, particularly for maintaining your child's behavior.

Many times, a desired behavior cannot be motivated by reinforcing a single response. This is due to a number of factors, such as the complexity of the behavior or the age and knowledge of the child. In such instances, I suggest the use of another operant conditioning principle called shaping.

Shaping a desired behavior involves reinforcing small steps toward a desired action rather than reinforcing only the desired response. The final desired behavior is eventually achieved through the reinforcement of each step, which eventually leads to the final response you were looking for. For example, if your child receives a failing grade in advanced algebra, she may need to improve her study habits before her grades increase. Therefore, in your attempt to raise your child's grade (your goal), you could set up a contingency schedule that reinforces a higher grade at the end of the semester ($5 for a C, $10 for a B, and $15 dollars for an A). Likewise, you can set up a shaping schedule composed of small steps to help ensure the goal is reached, such as reading a book on how to study, studying for one hour every day after school, and/or working on a computer program that teaches advanced algebra.

Another principle that pertains to motivation is termed self-fulfilling prophecy, or the Pygmalion Effect. In the mid-1960s, Drs. Rosenthal and Jacobson told the teachers of elementary age students, based on the results of an achievement test, some of the students in each class were "likely to show unusual intellectual gains in the year ahead." In fact, there was no measurable difference between the test scores of the students who the researchers labeled "superior" students and those of the other children. As Rosenthal and Jacobson anticipated, the students who had been labeled "potential achievers" showed significant gains in IQ. This finding was attributed to the notion teachers expected more of the students labeled as achievers. The researchers referred to this phenomenon as the Pygmalion Effect because "they felt that teachers' expectations had influenced the students to become intelligent in the same way the expectations of the mythical Greek sculptor Pygmalion had caused a statue he had carved to become endowed with life (Rosenthal and Jacobson, Pygmalion in the Classroom, 1968)."

The link between this concept and parenting is if parents communicate high expectations to a child he or she can make good decisions, do well in school, be hardworking, and so on, the likelihood the child will develop these positive traits will increase. The classic movie *My Fair Lady* illustrates the Pygmalion effect. Two different individuals in the movie treat a lowly flower girl, Eliza, differently. The effect of this treatment is revealed when the flower girl says to one of the characters in the movie, "I shall always be a flower girl to Professor Higgins because he always treats me as a flower girl, and always will, but I know I can be a lady to you, because you treat me as a lady, and always will."

It is true our children come to us with many strengths and shortcomings. I am convinced if I place less emphasis on their weaknesses and magnify their strengths in our conversations and in the way I treat them, eventually their strengths will overshadow their shortcomings.

Some related strategies (based on a psychological idea called operant conditioning) that have been used to discourage negative behavior and to reinforce positive behavior are allowances and token reward systems.

Allowance: I recommend each child receive a weekly allowance that is composed of both earned and unearned portions. Receiving the earned portion is contingent upon complying with some prescribed routine (i.e., Table 3a — Family Chore Chart) that has been agreed upon in advance. Meanwhile, the unearned portion is an amount of money the child receives irrespective of performance. Consistently receiving an unearned amount of money reminds the child much of what they get from parents is unearned. By paying the unearned portion, the parents also ensure the child will consistently receive money that can be used to cover some ongoing expenses. Making a portion of the allowance contingent upon performance teaches a work ethic and can be used as an incentive for healthy attitudes and actions.

Table 3a.
Family Chore Chart
For (Name of Responsible Person)

Chore/Activity	Mon	Tue	Wed	Thr	Fri	Sat
Make Bed	W	W	W	W	W	W
Clean Room	W	W	W	W	W	W
Feed the Dog or Cat	W	W	W	W	W	W
Take Trash & Recycle Bins to Street			W			
Return Recycle Bin to Garage			W			
Sweep Kitchen	Whenever Mom or Dad Ask (W)					
Load or Unload Dishwasher	Whenever Mom or Dad Ask (W)					
Vacuum Upstairs Hall						R
Sweep Garage						B
Extra Chores	Whenever Mom or Dad Ask (W)					

Directions: You must do your chores to receive an allowance. Every chore is worth a certain amount of money. You will be paid in chips during the week. You can turn these chips in for money on Saturdays. The type of chips you will receive for each chore is designated by W, R, or B. The chip values are: W=white chip, worth $1.00; R=red chip, worth $2.00; B=blue chip, worth $3.00, and NC=no chip. Whenever you do a chore, either collect a chip from Mom or Dad at bedtime or circle the chore on the chart and collect your chips all at once on Saturday.

Token Reward System: An effective strategy that employs frequent reinforcement as a means of motivation is the use of a token economy. This involves determining, in advance, what types of behaviors and attitudes will be reinforced, as well as the level of reinforcement. Every time a pre-designated behavior is performed by a child, that behavior is reinforced by a chip that can be turned in for a reward. Conversely, when the child disobeys a rule, a designated number of chips is forfeited.

Index Card Reinforcement System: Another version of the token system that has been used in a variety of settings is called the index card reinforcement system. This system involves writing reinforcers on 3x5 cards and then assigning behaviors to a certain number of cards. Once again, the defining characteristic of a reinforcer is its ability to increase the desired behavior it follows, like doing homework, obeying curfews, feeding the dog, making a bed, and so on.

A tool my wife and I have used to implement this system can be seen in Table 3b below. To implement the system, we simply transferred all of our family rules into column 1 of this table. After we listed our rules, we assigned a certain number of cards to each rule by recording a number in column 2. The number of cards was based on how important we, the parents, considered the rule to be. For example, we assigned more cards to a rule that has to do with safety, like "do not give your home address to strangers you meet on the Internet," and fewer cards to rules having to do with things like homework or making a bed before school.

Although it is more time consuming, we listed in column 3 the privileges our children were restricted from until they completed the tasks listed. It should be noted here the more a child acts out, the more specific you will need to be in articulating and enforcing consequences. This principle is discussed in more detail in the next chapter.

Table 3b.
Index Card Reinforcer Chart

Family Rules (Transfer All Family Rules to this Column, or Just the 5-10 Most Critical for Now)	Number of Reinforcer Cards (List the Number of Cards You Want to Assign to this Rule)	Lose All Privileges Until Tasks on the Reinforcer Cards Are Completed (Optional but Helpful for Parents with Bad Memories)

Directions: When you break a family rule listed in column 1, you will be required to complete the assigned number of cards listed in column 2. In column 3, we have listed the activities you will not be able to participate in until you complete your reinforcer cards.

17

CONTRACTING FOR PERFORMANCE

When you are raising a tween or teen with chronic behavior problems, you may want to consider contracting for desired performance. Although this technique can require considerable time, it works when less formal interventions fail. And, in reality, if interactions are failing, then it makes sense that the next steps would require more time and energy investments.

You can prepare a behavioral contract by 1) specifying all the expectations you have for your child, such as time to get out of bed in the morning, chores, restricted places or friends, and curfew; 2) stipulating the consequences of not complying with the contract; 3) informing your child of the contract and negotiating the terms of the contract, where appropriate; 4) signing the contract with your child; 5) following up to ensure the terms of the contract are complied with; and when they are not, 6) enforcing the consequences specified in the contract. While all of this sounds daunting, the chart below covers everything in a few boxes. The 'process' is more complex than the execution.

The following table will help guide you in developing a Parent/Child contract.

Table 4.
Parent/Child Contract

Contract between (names of parents and child):

Things I Will or Will Not Do	Benefits if I Do Comply	Consequences if I Do Not Comply

I agree to comply with all that is described in this contract. I also understand that if I do not comply with those things described in column 1, I will incur the negative consequences stated in column 3.

Child's Signature:

These contracts may seem rigid, but in many cases they are very helpful in bringing order to the life a young person who is out of control. If you are having great difficulty communicating with your child, you may want to enlist the help of a professional (counselor, psychologist) in negotiating these contracts. I have provided you with an example of such a filled in contract in Table 4.

If, in spite of your best efforts to persuade your child to comply with your family rules, your son or daughter continues to disregard your parental authority, you may want to seek help from your local Juvenile Justice department.

> CAVEAT: Yes, this IS a drastic step, so step carefully. Once you and your family is involved with the 'government', it becomes an entirely different structure, 100% governed by them. You lose much of your parental control to obtain some outside control. Think about this carefully, and even discuss it with your child and explain that some of their life will now be

controlled by an outside third party with the force of law to enforce it. Hopefully, this alone might help to right the boat.

Typically, to get their assistance you will need to file an "Unruly Child" complaint. In the state I am most familiar with, (Georgia), the definition of an unruly child is a child who is habitually and without justification truant from school; is habitually disobedient of the reasonable lawful commands of his or her parent(s), guardian(s), or other custodian(s), and is ungovernable; has committed an offense only applicable to a child; deserts his or her home; wanders or loiters about the streets between the hours of 12 midnight and 5 a.m.; patronizes bars; possesses alcoholic beverages; disobeys the terms of supervision contained in a court order; commits a delinquent act, and is in need of supervision, treatment, or rehabilitation.

If your child fits this definition, I strongly urge you to consider contacting your local Department of Juvenile Justice, but with the caveat above equally strongly considered. This may seem like a harsh approach to parenting. However, my experience tells me that, in some cases, it is the only way to get a young person's attention and send the message he or she is required by law to accept reasonable parental supervision and direction. In so doing, both parents must agree to, and be willing to see through, the process.

Of course, your child will complain profusely, not realizing you are taking these measures to save his or her future, and even his or her life, in many cases. Such complaints should be ignored, just as your child has ignored your parental demands to comply with family rules.

My advice to parents who have trouble ignoring their child's unfounded pleas for mercy and who tend to give in to their child's demands is to say things like, "toughen up" or "buy a helmet." This is meant to communicate the message parenting can be very difficult at times, and rather than walking away from the challenge, you need to take whatever measures are appropriate to bring things under control with the understanding that the sooner you intervene, the better. Hoping or praying or wondering things to improve is wonderful and a great way to spend your personal time AFTER you get down to the business of fixing your problem or making a plan to work with professionals to help fix your problem.

18

EVALUATING PERFORMANCE

THIS SECTION INCLUDES MILESTONES, METRICS, MEASURING PROGRESS, baseline, and status checks for performance because performance is everything. Evaluating performance is key to the success of your Family Management Plan because a perfectly designed and administered plan is a waste of time and energy if it is not implemented as planned. To do this requires some understanding of performance standards and how they apply to the process of evaluating your child's/children's performance.

Performance standards are those expectations you have concerning how you want your child to perform a task, such as study for a test, wash the car, mow the lawn, practice the piano, or wash the dishes. When you evaluate a child's performance, you compare what you want or expect the performance to be (the performance standard) to what you actually observe it to be. If there is a considerable discrepancy (shortfall) between what you want and what you get, in the way of performance, then your child is underperforming. Or, in simpler terms, your child isn't doing what is expected.

However, this may or may not be the child's fault. For example, if you consistently set a bad example by not performing at the level you expect your children to perform (i.e., you tell them to make their beds and you never make yours), it is likely they will perform at the level of your example rather than performing in accordance with your stated expectations. So, this means that "do as I say, not as I do" isn't going to work.

Poor performance can also result when you do not clearly describe, and in most cases demonstrate, what you expect your child to do. In such cases, you are mostly to blame for poor performance because your children should not be expected to read your thoughts and guess what you want them to do. They should know precisely what you expect.

For example, in washing the dishes, you can say, "please do the dishes," but if you don't provide specific visual instructions as to what that means, then don't expect them to be clean, soap free, or stacked so they don't fall down like a house of cards. Have your child stand next to you while you do a few dishes and explain, "no food left on the plate, also do the backs, no soap left, then put on the stacker largest plates in the back and smallest in the front". The, stand next to your child while s/he does the next five plates. Correct as necessary, but don't be overbearing. The next day, leave the child to do the job alone and check it afterward, and then comment.

Another cause of poor performance can be partly due to not being organized. For example, if you ask your 12-year-old son to mow the lawn and you provide him with an old decrepit lawn mower that he must push up and down a steep hill, it is likely you will get a relatively poor performance–if your son performs at all. Once again you are to blame, because if you want good results, you need to provide your children with the resources they need to perform at a high level.

If, however, you make a practice to explicitly state, even write down, what you want in the way of performance, demonstrate how you want your child to perform, and provide your child what he or she needs to perform at the expected level, then the child must shoulder the responsibility for poor performance. In other words, only after you have taken all excuses away from your child by carefully explaining and demonstrating what you want done, and providing the equipment or environment in which to do it, can you legitimately hold the child accountable for not doing what he or she is capable of doing (assuming the child has the necessary intellect and strength to do what you want done). The key here is to explicitly state your expectations so your child has no uncertainty about what you want him or her to accomplish.

One more point here.

If you know how your child learns best, use that method for these projects. Some learn best by reading, so write the instructions down. Those who learn best by listening, then talk. Kinesthetic kids learn best by doing…let them do. And so on.

Another key in evaluating performance is to discipline yourself to follow up and both 1) evaluate performance by comparing what you expect to what you want, and 2) if there is a discrepancy, hold the child accountable and require him or her to do better next time until the task is performed correctly. Letting your child off the hook when he or she is capable of performing at a level that meets your expectations only teaches your child the bad habit of underperforming. This habit is difficult to overcome and can carry into adulthood.

Follow up and evaluation are integral parts of any family intervention, policy, or procedure you may develop or implement as a result of reading this book. Consequently, rather than developing a separate evaluation tool here, I have incorporated these concepts into the various tools I have recommended you use.

19

BUILDING AND MAINTAINING HEALTHY RELATIONSHIPS

ALTHOUGH RULES AND CORRESPONDING DISCIPLINARY MEASURES ARE critical when communicating to your tweens and teens your expectations and the consequences of noncompliance, a parenting strategy that only relies on rules is missing a key ingredient. Perhaps the most important thing you can do to influence your children is to build a personal relationship with each of them.

According to a number experts (renowned experts John Gottman, Willard Harley, and Vincent Covello have all published in this area), the emotional feeling an individual has toward another person is called relationship sentiment. In many ways, relationship sentiment is like a bank account. If you have positive sentiment, it is like having a positive balance in your relationship account. Similarly, if you have a negative sentiment balance, your relationship is moving in the wrong direction. With this in mind, it is important that family members be deliberate about the way they treat each other so they can cooperate and work together toward building positive sentiment. The more positive sentiment the relationship has, the more likely a family will enjoy their relationship and want to spend time together. In simple English, when you communicate sincerely and openly, without judgment and negativity, you are building your relationship with your children. You know that already as a parent.

The matrix below will help you practice building sentiment among family members. For example, you and your spouse should have a very brief conversation each evening where you ask him or her to tell you what you said or did during the day that was upsetting. Write these things down and then, working separately, write down a self-imposed consequence for your offense, and something you will commit to do differently to avoid the offense in the future. Do not argue or go into any deep discussion. Keep focused on what you have done to offend your spouse and what you can do to change.

If this discussion and 'list' gets too deep, or too long, then only ask for the most obvious or most egregious, or most upsetting thing you did during the day. Limiting this discussion to one thing will permit you to escape with your life, and in a reasonable time frame (15 minutes). This is not intended to be a grief inducing session, and certainly not on a nightly basis.

Once you master this process as a couple, you can assign two siblings who are having difficulties go through the same process. In fact, one of your consequences for disobeying a rule could be to use the Sentiment Building Guide, see below, for one week. In either case, an adult should facilitate the activity to make sure it goes smoothly. Once again, the point is to teach family members how to build good interpersonal relationships.

NEGATIVE SENTIMENT TRACKING			
Day of the Week	Things I Said or Did That Had a Negative Effective on Our Relationship Sentiment (This is according to my Brother/Sister/Parent)	My Self-Imposed Consequences	What I Will Say or Do Differently to Counter Negative Sentiment (1N-3P)
Mon			
Tue			
Wed			
Thur			
Fri			
Sat			
Sun			

POSITIVE SENTIMENT TRACKING							
Monitoring	Mon	Tue	Wed	Thur	Fri	Sat	Sun
Things I Said or Did That Helped Our Relationship Sentiment (This is according to my Brother/Sister/Parent)							
My Self-Imposed Rewards							

Parents who have unconditional love toward their children prize and warmly accept each child without placing stipulations on the acceptance. They do not have an attitude that says, "I'll accept you when you do well in school, or when you hit a home run in baseball, or when you clean up the house." Rather, these parents communicate to each child he or she is free to choose an individual course in life without risking the loss of acceptance. The child should know the parent will continue to love and accept them regardless of their success or performance.

Empathy refers to the capacity you have to feel another person's feelings. A parent who has an accurate empathic understanding will sense a child's feelings as if they were his or her own, but without getting lost in the child's experience. This response requires close and ongoing contact with each child and serious reflection on what the child is experiencing, and how you would feel and react if you were at the same age and in the same situation. With this type of understanding, you are in a much better position to sensitively guide your children through the difficult decisions they must make as they grow older.

Maintaining an accurate empathic understanding can be a challenge because as adults we invariably forget what it is like to be children. We tend to look at the world from our own perspective and forget things can look very different from the vantage point of a child or teenager.

A genuine parent does not put on a false front. Rather, a genuine parent can be trusted to "say what he or she means and mean what he or she says." A genuine parent openly and honestly expresses both negative and positive emotions toward a child without losing control or saying things that are better left unsaid.

As I have stated above, to meet these three conditions of a good relationship, it is important to spend time with and communicate with your children about things they like to discuss. To ensure that my wife and I spend adequate time with our children, we help them identify activities they have a passion for and attempt to build a relationship, even a lifestyle, around these activities.

For example, to ensure I developed a good relationship with my older children, I started riding bicycles. We bought bicycles and all the riding equipment (e.g., tight shorts and shirts, cool sunglasses, helmets), signed up for a bike ride across the state of Georgia, invited friends and neighbors to join us, and then rode our bikes 457 miles in a week's time (ouch!). This adventure led to many other long rides and untold memories with my family. It also led to multiple chiropractic visits, but that is the price of being engaged with your family and children.

On these long adventures, we solidified relationships and taught our children many important lessons about life. When our youngest son came onto the scene, we realized quickly he did *not* like riding bikes. Finally, after great anguish about how we might develop a relationship with this high energy boy who loved hanging out with his friends and skateboarding, we discovered he loves horses. So, my wife and I decided to build a relationship with him around this interest. We first purchased a very safe, inexpensive horse. We identified a friend who allowed us to keep the horse at his ranch for a minimal cost. Identifying an inexpensive horse and a temporary place to keep her allowed us to test our son's commitment to horses with minimal investment on our part.

To make a long story short, we now have a small horse farm, nine horses. Our eldest daughter gives horseback riding lessons, and our youngest son, Jordan, the target of our intervention, is a professional calf-roper on the rodeo circuit. All this came from a concerted effort to help our son. This experience has reinforced our belief that it is much easier to parent and teach a child when we are playing and working together. This idea is summed up by a billboard sign I once saw: "Children spell love: T-I-M-E." When you invest time in your child, you will develop a relationship that will carry you through the difficult times.

To further invest in relationships among family members, we have set aside one night a week as family night. On this night (held on Mondays), we all get together and talk, go bowling, ride horses or four-wheelers, go to nice restaurants, etc. We also plan to start these evenings with a formal discussion on a topic of interest. We have discussed things like table manners, how to prevent electrocution (do not leave our hairdryer plugged in and laying in the sink), drugs and alcohol, dates, music, and sex, to name a few. Once again, the goal of these meetings is to bring the family together to build our relationships and to provide a forum for my wife and I to pass along what we want our children to know and do to become healthy, happy, responsible adults.

We also believe family vacations are a must in building family relationships. They give the family time to regroup without friends around. As with every other family activity, we feel like vacations should be planned in advance with input from all family members. This is especially important with teenagers.

The implications of Dr. Roger's teachings are that to be an effective parent, you must develop a good, healthy relationship with each child. Although this takes time and effort (like playing basketball or going fishing or taking a walk), the payoff is great in the teen years when your child's outlook on life begins to change.

As was discussed at the beginning of this section, a defining characteristic of a functional family is the presence of order in the home. The parenting strategy outlined in this section has provided you with ideas about how to develop a Family Parenting Plan that can be used to 1) develop a family identity statement and mascot, i.e., "brand" your family, 2) develop family goals and a goal statement, 3) decide which activities family members will engage in to achieve these goals, 4) set rules to support goals and activities, 5) justify rules, 6) select, assign, and administer appropriate consequences, 7) administer discipline appropriately, 8) motivate compliance with family rules, 9) contract for performance, 10) evaluate performance, and 11) develop and maintain a healthy relationship with each child. (Yes, this is way more than some parents and some families can handle, at first or at all. So, don't push yourself so hard. Choose the primary and high points in each area and focus on them. You will be 99% ahead of every other family regardless.)

The next section will discuss principles that must be understood to effectively implement your Family Management Plan.

20

PRINCIPLES OF GOOD INTERPERSONAL COMMUNICATION

INTERPERSONAL COMMUNICATION IS KEY TO EVERY ASPECT OF developing, implementing, and evaluating an effective parenting plan. In fact, lack of communication and miscommunication are the hallmarks of a dysfunctional family. In view of the need to communicate effectively, your Family Management Plan should include guidelines for communication. For example, the FMP could address communication as an area of focus by developing plans for achieving consistent family communication and effective interpersonal communication. These goals could be accomplished by teaching each family member the principles of good interpersonal communication, respectively.

Regularly scheduled family meetings can provide you with the family time required to develop and implement your FMP. For example, we have used these meetings as a time to resolve family conflicts, plan vacations, obtain feedback on our FMP, and instruct our children on a number of topics, ranging from personal hygiene to drug use. Perhaps the most important reason for holding these meetings on a consistent basis is to demonstrate to your children that you value family communication. Some guidelines for holding family councils are as follows:

1. Meet on a regularly scheduled basis.
2. Plan ahead by setting an agenda.
3. Establish ground rules to ensure order, such as "only one person will speak at a time," and "all comments, including negative comments, must be made in a respectful manner."
4. Decisions made can be voted on with the parents reserving the right to veto decisions they feel are not in the best interest of the family or a particular family member.
5. Begin the session on a positive note.
6. Strive to include everyone by giving each participant a meaningful assignment.
7. Although parents should always preside, children should have the opportunity to participate and should be allowed to offer suggestions that are taken seriously. (This is a chance to help them to feel heard and feel like they have a voice. It can be instrumental in their stake in the game, rather than disconnecting from an activity they don't like doing.)
8. Do not allow the meeting to degenerate into a gripe session. However, each member of the family should be free to openly and respectfully express his or her feelings on the issues being considered by the council.
9. Practice good communication skills during the council. These skills are described in some detail in a later chapter.

Be patient if your meeting gets off track, particularly if members of your family are communicating in positive ways. (You can't always define success ahead of time; sometimes you have to pivot. Remember your greater over-arching goals and not just your initial goals.) Since the very essence of a family meeting is family communication, I consider our meeting a success even if nothing else is accomplished besides good communication among family members.

As was mentioned above, a good way to keep your family meetings on track is to set an agenda. Some agenda items we have included in our family council agenda are as follows:

1. Review calendar and correlate upcoming activities.
2. Plan weekly family activity.
3. Assign or clarify chores, such as clean the main level or upstairs bathroom; mow or trim yard, hoe the garden, weed the yard; wash breakfast, lunch, or dinner dishes; wash doors, woodwork, walls, or windows; dust furniture; take out trash; vacuum downstairs, main level, or upstairs; shop for groceries; sweep the garage and sidewalks; etc.
4. Review a "family standard" or the expectations concerning family rules.
5. Communicate and discuss a new or existing item in the Family Management Plan.
6. Teach a lesson/principle from one of the topic areas included in the next section of the book.
7. Read a book.
8. Eat snacks together. (Never underestimate the bonding power of good food!)

One thing you may want to consider adding to your family meeting is the idea of an Activity Request Form, a very useful tool for improving communication through advanced planning. At one point in the process of raising our children, my wife and I were experiencing many last-minute requests to do things like go to the movies, go skating, spend the night, and so on. This was frustrating because if we did not give our children permission, they would get upset. If we did give into their pleading, we typically had to make adjustments in our own schedule to accommodate their last-minute request. In other words, their last-minute emergency requests turned into our problem.

To overcome this problem, I devised an Activity Request Form which I presented at our weekly family meeting. This planning form, when used on a consistent basis, helps alleviate last-minute requests and places the burden of planning on our children instead of on the parents. It also teaches children to think and plan ahead, which often results in a much better activity. This is not to say it is wrong to be spontaneous. It can be great fun to plan an activity at the last minute. However, if you want to simplify your life and bring order to your family, giving in to last-minute requests should be the exception rather than the rule.

Oftentimes, communication needs to be one-on-one to be most effective. This is particularly true when discussing sensitive matters or administering discipline. It is helpful to schedule personal interviews with your children on a regular basis. For example, have a standing date with your son or daughter every week or every month (e.g., every Wednesday or the first Sunday of every month). This can be a time when you develop a close relationship with your child by sharing intimate details about problems, concerns, hopes, aspirations, and so on. If you establish this tradition early on in your child's life, it will become a habit.

To further improve communication, you should take the time to learn about your child's interests and those things he or she is most passionate about. Does your child like music? If yes, learn what types of music he or she prefers, and who the artists are, including such things as their hit records and how they became popular. Along the same lines, most teenagers like movies. If you learn something about their favorite actors, you are in a position to carry on a conversation that will interest them.

You may ask yourself, "Why would I want to learn about these things, especially if I don't like the types of music or movies my children like?" At such times, remember this is not about you and your interests. Rather, it is about discovering what your child is interested in and making a point to talk about these things, so he or she is willing and interested in talking to you.

Though... very often children are keenly interested in the things their parents 'do' in their spare time, their interests, what kinds of books they read, sports they play, movies THEY see, and music THEY listen to, or listened to when they were the age of their children. These conversations will, as often as not, then segue into the children's interests in these areas, opening up a potentially closed discussion of 'why do you want to know?'

My speaking about your own teen and tween experiences and interests, you also show that you aren't some ancient gargoyle, but an equally interesting person your children should want to know better.

Communication requires a sense of timing. For example, many young people are not ready to talk about "the events of the day" right after school. When our four older children were in high school, they often brought friends over on weekends and we all talked late into the night. Many times those late night talks were very revealing with regard to the concerns and ambitions of our teenagers and their friends. Why? Because that is when our kids and their friends wanted to talk and so we (typically my wife) met them on their own terms.

Another good way to encourage communication is to take walks with your children. Our family lives near a park where we like to take a daily 3-mile walk around the 1.5-mile walking trail. These walks were especially helpful for one of our teenagers, who would tend to vent his issues and concerns about life for the first 1.5 miles, and then laugh and talk about all sorts of things during the second half of the walk. I learned to simply listen and withhold advice and judgment during lap one, and then enjoy the conversation the second time around.

Our third son loves to fish. So how might I engage him in a conversation? If you guessed that I ask him a fishing related question, you are right. Another way to get his undivided attention is to ask him if he wants to rent a boat and go fishing.

When giving advice to our children, I attempt to accentuate the positive. For example, tell them what they should do instead of what they should not do. Say, for example, "Wear your helmet each time you ride your horse." Do not say, "Do not ride your horse without a safety helmet."

When I feel a need to give advice to one of our older children, it is typically given sparingly and usually takes the form of questions such as, "Have you thought about this, that, or the other?" or "Have you tried this, or that alternative?" I have found that communication usually shuts down when I get into a "You should do this" or "You should do that" mode.

Sharing feelings, especially negative emotions such as anger, sorrow, embarrassment, and fear, can be difficult at times. There is much "emotional baggage" that goes along with negative feelings. When your children become teenagers, they will know how to effectively exploit your weaknesses and hit your "hot buttons," so to speak. This is why it is so important to understand and apply sound communication principles when relating to your children.

21

MESSAGE MAPPING: A STRATEGY FOR COMMUNICATING AROUND HIGH CONCERN ISSUES

AS A PSYCHOTHERAPIST I AM OFTENTIMES ASKED BY PARENTS TO HELP them through very difficult situations. And, more often than not, these situations involve teenagers. As today's children are often growing up faster than previous generations, these difficult issues now swoop down into the pre-teen/tween age ranges. Is it ever too young to discuss drugs or sex or abusive behavior?

A tool that has helped parents communicate more effectively about high concern issues like drugs, dating, sex, STDs, abortion, legal issues, and any other potentially volatile or sensitive topics is called Message Mapping. This is a structured process that generates a "message map" that can be used by parents in preparing for and engaging in important conversations with their children.

In simple terms, it is a visual aid that provides, at a glance, the parent's messages for high concern or controversial issues.

Developing and using message maps can achieve several important parenting communication goals, including 1) anticipating your children's questions and concerns around difficult issues before these issues are raised, 2) organizing your thinking and developing prepared messages in response to anticipated questions and concerns, 3) developing supporting facts and proofs for each key message, and 4) promoting open dialogue about messages both inside and outside your family. Thus, the message map is a tool for parents to know, in advance, what they want to say about a particular subject and be able to make sure they hit all the key points and don't miss anything, including the responses to most teens' response/arguments, and to have it in a way they can refer to it and stay on message.

The process parents use to generate message maps can be as important as the end product. Message mapping exercises often reveal fundamentally differing viewpoints between parents in how each would respond to the same question, issue, or concern. If these differing viewpoints are not clarified and agreed upon by both parents in advance of dealing with difficult parenting issues, parents can send conflicting messages. The savvy teenager will see these inconsistencies and manipulate them toward his or her own goals, which are oftentimes not in the teen's best interest. This is why parents should sit down together to develop message maps around important issues that relate to family values, identity, and personal habits, first, before presenting to the teenager in question.

Several steps are involved in constructing a message map. The first step is to identify a complete list of your children's questions and concerns. The fact is, most questions that will be raised related to a controversy or concern can be anticipated. Here are some anticipated questions: "Hey Dad, what's wrong with using marijuana or drinking alcohol?" "Hey Mom, why can't I date college guys? I am sixteen." "What's wrong with having sex with my boyfriend?" "Why can't I go to an overnight party at the lake?" "Why can't I spend the night at my girlfriend's house?"

Most concerns expressed by young people and their peers are associated with a limited number of underlying issues about relationships with their peers, dating, sex, substance use, academics, religion, health and safety, appearance, money, equity/fairness, honesty and trust, parental control, and accountability.

The second step in message map construction is to organize your thinking and develop prepared messages in response to anticipated questions and concerns. That is, develop three key messages in response to each of the questions you have listed in the first step. Key messages are typically developed through brainstorming with your spouse or with a therapist or pastor or grandparent. The brainstorming session produces a message narrative, which, in turn, is reduced to key messages that can be entered on the message map. And while you likely could create a dozen different responses, the object here is simplicity and clarity, both of which can be accomplished with brevity.

According to Dr Vincent Covello, a renowned expert in message mapping exercises, mental noise theory states that when people (your kids) are upset, they often have difficulty hearing, understanding, and remembering information. Mental noise can reduce a person's ability to process information by over 80 percent. The challenge for parents, therefore, is 1) to overcome the barriers that mental noise creates, 2) to produce accurate messages, and 3) to achieve maximum communication effectiveness within the constraints posed by mental noise. Parents must strive for concise, brief, and clear messages. And, of course, they also have to be presented in a calm and positive manner, sharing information as opposed to shoving it down your children's throats.

Solutions to mental noise theory that guide key message development specifically, and message mapping generally, include:

- Developing a limited number of key messages: ideally three key messages or one key message with three parts, for each underlying concern or specific question (conciseness).
- Keeping individual key messages brief: less than 9 words for each key message and/or less than 27 words for the entire set of three key messages (brevity).
- Developing messages that are clearly understood by your children: typically at the grade readability level that is most appropriate for your child (clarity).

Additional solutions include:

- Placing messages within a message set so the most important messages occupy the first and last positions.
- Developing key messages that cite credible third parties.
- Using graphics and other visual aids to enhance key messages. For example, use graphic images or videos of the effects of tobacco on the body and/or injuries sustained by drunk drivers.
- Balancing negative key messages with positive, constructive, or solution-oriented key messages. This is based on the 1N=3P rule. This communication rule is based on research revealing that for every negative interaction between two people, it takes at least three positive interactions to restore the relationship to where it was before the negative transaction occurred.
- Avoiding unnecessary uses of the words no, not, never, nothing, none.

The third step in message map construction is to develop supporting facts and proofs for each key message. The same principles that guide key message construction should guide the development of supporting information.

The fourth step in the process is to prepare to use the map. This means you should study and practice the use of each message map before delivering the messages to your children.

In addition to the four steps and principles just described, it is important to keep this adage in mind during the communication process: "People want to know you care before they care what you know."

To account for this principle, you will note in the following examples that a message map includes a space for an opening statement. This statement should express a sense of caring, such as, "I would first like to say I value you very much and want the best for you now and in the future." This type of introduction to any conversation around a sensitive topic tends to increase the likelihood that the listener (your son or daughter) will actually pay attention to what you have to say. Or, if you think something a tiny bit more 'hammer on the head' would get and keep their attention, try, "I want to first say this whole activity is designed to achieve one thing… you still being here and alive and well six months from now, a year from now, and to live long enough for me to become a grandparent. Keeping you alive is my responsibility and I take it very seriously."

Examples of this four-step process can be seen in Tables 5a and 5b. I have added background statements to each example so you will have some context for the map and how it was used.

Table 5a.
Message Map on a Question about Sex

Background (this section is not included in a message map. I have included it to help set the context for this map): This is a map used by a Sunday school teacher who was challenged with the following question and statement.
Question: What's wrong with having sex before marriage? All the kids at school have sex.
Opening Statement: During our lesson last week, Laura asked a very serious question. It's such an important question I said I would take time to answer it in this week's lesson. Before I begin, let me say that the reason I took extra time to prepare my response is because I care deeply about each of you and believe you deserve a well-thought-out answer.

Message 1: There are many advantages to delaying sex.	Message 2: Engaging in sex at a young age can have serious irreversible consequences.	Message 3: There are many things you can do on a date besides engage in sexual activity.
Supporting Fact 1A: Dating without sex gives you time to learn how to discern sexual motives and avoid sexual exploitation.	Supporting Fact 2A: Most relationships between teenagers don't last, whereas most serious consequences do last.	Supporting Fact 3A: Dating is fun and is designed to allow you time to get to know people of the opposite sex, such as how they think and what they like to do.
Supporting Fact 1B: Delaying sex can reduce the likelihood that you will get a sexually transmitted disease or AIDS.	Supporting Fact 2B: Sexually transmitted diseases (STDs) like herpes, venereal warts, and HIV are incurable.	Supporting Fact 3B: Instead of worrying about the pressure of sex on a date, consider these activities: exercising together (riding bikes or jogging), going to a concert, going to a movie, taking a hike, having a picnic, going shopping, talking about your goals and dreams, taking dance lessons.
Supporting Fact 1C: Waiting to have sex until you are married builds self-discipline and ensures that you will not infect your life partner with a disease.	Supporting Fact 2C: If you do engage in sexual relations before marriage, you run a greater risk of becoming pregnant or causing a pregnancy, and/or performing poorly in school–or dropping out of school due to infection or pregnancy.	Supporting Fact 3C: There are so many things to do that are fun without the pressure of sex and all that comes with it. You can talk about what you will be doing in 10 years, your dreams, goals and life aspirations.

Table 5a: Message Map on a Question about Sex

If time allows, present the key messages and supporting information contained in a message map using the Triple T Model: 1) Tell your child what you are going to tell them, i.e., key messages; 2) Tell them more, i.e., supporting information; (3) Tell them again what you told them, i.e., repeat key messages.

Again, it is important you study and practice the use of message maps before delivering them to your children. This will allow you to take advantage of opportunities to re-emphasize or bridge to key messages when you are addressing a variety of questions in a difficult conversation.

When using your maps, do your best to stay on the prepared messages in the message map; avoid "winging it". By staying on task, you will see through the "smoke and mirrors" created by your child's resistance.

Perhaps most important in this process is to be honest. Always tell the truth. Nothing undermines your credibility faster than lying.

In conclusion, message maps are a viable tool for parents who place a high priority on effective communication related to serious issues that they will invariably face when raising teenagers. Using these maps better ensures that information discussed around difficult issues has the optimum chance of being heard, understood, and remembered.

Table 5b: Issues Surrounding Underage Drinking & Driving

Table 5b.
Issues Surrounding Underage Drinking & Driving

Background (this section is not included in a message map. I have included it to help set the context for this map): This conversation took place in my office between a father and his son. The 17-year-old son had come home from a party with the smell of alcohol on his breath. The father called me and wanted me to talk to his son about the dangers of drinking and driving. I asked the father to come in for a session before bringing his son to the office. I assigned the father to work with the boy's mother (parents are divorced) in preparing a message map. I explained that they (the mom and dad) would be doing most of the talking. I reviewed the process of developing a map, and they went away with the agreement they would work together to prepare messages in anticipation to the following dialogue and question. The map they brought to the office the next week is outlined below. They met with me for about 15 minutes before their unsuspecting son came into the room. By the time their son entered the session, his parents were prepared and did a brilliant job of articulating their answers to his questions.

Anticipated Question and Comments: I don't see what the big deal is with what I did. My parents are overreacting. I only had one beer before I drove home from the party. I was in total control. What's wrong with having one drink before driving?

Opening Statement: The father said: "Son, your mother and I love you and want what's best for you."

Message 1: It's against the law.	Message 2: It's dangerous.	Message 3: It's harmful and addictive.
Supporting Fact 1A: We have no tolerance laws in our state.	Supporting Fact 2A: Each year 5,000 teens ages 16 to 20 die due to fatal injuries caused in a car crash (male deaths are 1.5 times higher than female deaths).	Supporting Fact 3A: The most serious effect of teenage drinking is it leads to adult dependence. The National Institute on Alcohol Abuse reports that teens who start drinking before the age of 15 are 4 times more likely to develop an alcohol addiction than those who don't.
Supporting Fact 1B: If you had been pulled over, you would have gone to jail for at least one day.	Supporting Fact 2B: Thirty-one percent of drivers 15 to 20 who died in traffic accidents had been drinking.	Supporting Fact 3B: Alcohol may also serve as a "gateway drug" into more serious drug use.
Supporting Fact 1C: If your breath results were over .08, you would have been fined, your license would have been completely suspended for one year, and you would have been required to complete 40 hours of community service.	Supporting Fact 2C: Each year, 400,000 teens are seriously injured in car accidents.	Supporting Fact 3C: Alcohol poisoning can cause a person to go into a coma or it can cause death.

22

COUNSELING YOUR CHILDREN

PRIVATE, ONE-ON-ONE COMMUNICATION IS OFTEN CALLED COUNSELING. My experience has been that many think they do it well, without training. The fact is, most people can counsel, but it does require knowledge and skills to transform a one-way monologue into a two-way dialogue. In short, the "counselor" (you, the parent) must learn to speak in a way that ensures the "counselee" (your tween or teen) will listen and, in way that ensures s/he will respond, creating a two way conversation and the progress necessary to a resolution.

As with communication, the ability to counsel your children is key to implementing and evaluating your parenting plan. Counseling can be quite effective if the proper principles are applied. These include 1) meeting one-on-one in a private setting, 2) letting your child do most of the talking, 3) listening to all your child has to say, 4) keeping what is said confidential, 5) striving to make your child understand you are hearing everything he or she says by repeating back—in your own words—what you think he or she said, 6) being patient and remaining calm and collected regardless of what is said (If you get upset, communication will stop and you will have to work to regain the trust of your child), and 7) making appropriate suggestions in a sensitive way.

If you want to be an effective counselor to your children, you must be an effective listener. Why? Because if you do not carefully listen to what your child is saying, you will not gain a good understanding of the causes and severity of any given problem. Without this, it is nearly impossible to give counsel.

I like to follow a six-step process when counseling my children. These steps are: 1) listening to understand the problem, how severe it is, and how long it has persisted; 2) paraphrasing what I have heard to reassure the child I am listening and to determine whether I understand what they are saying; 3) asking what he/she thinks is causing the problem; 4) asking what he/she can do to overcome the problem; 5) asking what he/she thinks others can do to help; and 6) providing guidance that will allow him/her to make decisions in full view of the possible consequences. I believe if you love your children, you will not allow them to make self-destructive decisions without bringing the consequences of these decisions to their attention. In view of this, I often point out to our children that, although they are free to make decisions throughout their lives, they will typically have very little control over the consequences.

These sessions should be held in a private setting and should provide an opportunity for your child to do most of the talking. Parents who insist on doing all the talking and demand what their children say in return is consistent with what the parent wants to hear typically shut down communication altogether. They simply teach their child how to say what they, the parents, want to hear instead of what the child is actually thinking or wants to say.

If you want to truly communicate with your child, you need to speak in a way your child will listen, and listen in a way your child will speak. Any other approach may give temporary relief, but inevitably causes a breakdown in communication.

To encourage my children to talk about a variety of things I want to monitor during a counseling session, I have a list of items I usually go over, such as school, teachers, friends, family, hobbies, favorite things to do, problems, and so on. Yes, this is an extensive list and you might decide to choose one or two of the list for each time you meet, covering the entire gamut of needs within a month's time.

I review these items in a regularly scheduled, private meeting with each child. If things are going well for a child, the private meetings can occur about one a month. When things are not going well, I meet with the struggling child on a more frequent basis.

With older teenagers, it is more difficult to schedule formal meetings. However, with some planning, you can set the stage for a teachable counseling session. In my case, this type of session occurred during a one-on-one game of basketball, when riding horses in the woods, while walking on the beach, and while attending concerts together. The point is, whenever your children really like to talk, you should be prepared to listen and provide feedback.

23

MEDIATING CONFLICTS

Just as mediation skills are required in a business setting to bring two parties together on a particular issue, mediation is also required in parenting. In fact, at times it seems like conflict mediation (diffusing arguments) is our most common parenting activity. This is particularly true when we are in close quarters, such as traveling in a car, or sitting together in a family meeting.

The primary purpose of mediation is to help your children come to an amicable resolution when they are in conflict. The mediation strategy I recommend is described here in the chart below.

Conflict Mediation Strategy

- Meet separately with the children who are in conflict.
- Listen carefully to both sides of the argument.
- Solicit and discuss possible solutions to the conflict.
- Attempt to get both sides to agree to a solution. If not, decide on a solution and enlist the support of both sides.
- Specify consequences that will result if the conflict flares up again.

- Agree to meet again to discuss progress.
- Reward progress and/or apply consequences to non-compliant child.

Conflict Mediation Strategy
- Meet separately with the children who are in conflict. - Listen carefully to both sides of the argument. - Solicit and discuss possible solutions to the conflict. - Attempt to get both sides to agree to a solution. If not, decide on a solution and enlist the support of both sides. - Specify consequences that will result if the conflict flares up again. - Agree to meet again to discuss progress. - Reward progress and/or apply consequences to non-compliant child.

24

INTRODUCTION TO TEACHING SESSIONS

Professional teachers play a critical role in the lives of our youth. However, their academic training does not touch on many of the things children must know to ensure their success in life. This is where a parent plays such a crucial training role.

To be effective in your role as a teacher, it is important to understand and apply correct principles in deciding what to teach and how to teach these things. To help you do these things effectively, I have provided you with the following: 1) a list of possible topics you may want to cover, the main ones, in my opinion, are in the text, and the rest are in the Appendix, 2) a tool that can help you systematically decide which topics you will teach, 3) a description of a variety of teaching methods you can use, 4) information pertaining to developmental and psychological considerations in teaching, 5) guidance on how to develop a lesson plan around a particular topic, and 6) some sample lesson plans and lesson ideas (Table 6) you can either teach or use as examples of how to prepare your own lesson plans. I have also provided a number of principles you should be familiar with when teaching.

25

DECIDING WHAT TO TEACH

IN THE FIRST SECTION OF THE BOOK, I EXPLAINED THE STEPS OF creating a Family Management Plan. Just like with family management, the first step I recommend that you take in your efforts to teach your children to have good health and character is to systematically plan what you will teach by developing a Family Teaching Plan (FTP). Yes, one more "Plan", but success does require planning. Your FTP will function as the equivalent to a business training manual. While businesses formulate training plans that include all the training needs of their employees and the training activities they will employ to meet these needs, an FTP should include the things you want your children to know and do so they can be healthy, safe, and live up to their potential as individuals, members of your/their family, and members of society at-large.

I recommend a five-step process for developing an FTP.

Step 1 requires listing those things you want your children to know, that is, what you want to teach them. To complete this step, you and your spouse should brainstorm all the basic life lessons you want your children to learn. Start with the big things, like "visualizing a safe and healthy, cooperative family," and move toward the smaller things, like "visualize looking both ways before crossing the street." Obviously, these things will vary depending on the age of your children. In any case, you should go through this process of deciding what to teach on a regularly scheduled basis to make sure you are teaching those things that are best suited to the needs and age of each child. To help you get started, I have provided you with an extensive list of topics you may want to cover. This list is displayed in Table 6.

It is important to note that I have gone way beyond the usual list of things you might want to 'teach' your children at this point. And yes, there is a curriculum section for each of them in the book.

But, I have chosen the ten I believe are the most common and important topics and those will be in the main part of the book itself. The other 15 or 18 or so topics I have detailed will appear in the Appendix. They are no less important nor should be shuffled off to the side. It is just that the recommendation or the book is not to overwhelm parents with a few dozen teaching topics. Limit them to the ones most parents are concerned about… sex, drugs, honesty, family safety, respect within the family unit, etc.

You are free to choose any, all, or none of these topics. Though, I would have to recommend you at least consider the ones in the part of the book following this section. If you have the time and interest, or your children want to learn more about a specific topic, go for it!

While on a recent retreat to the mountains to celebrate our 25th wedding anniversary, my wife and I went through the process of deciding what we want to teach our 9-year-old and 16-year-old sons before they graduate from high school. Obviously, they are at very different stages, so we considered each boy separately. To organize our thinking about what we want them to know and do, we discussed their needs in terms of five dimensions important to their health and well-being: social, physical, intellectual, emotional, and spiritual. This organizing framework is based on my beliefs that 1) all people are multi-dimensional beings, 2) we all have needs in these areas, and 3) these needs must be satisfied to ensure that we have good health and well-being. (Please note I have provided a sample lesson plan, Acquiring The Dimensions of Health and Well-Being, in the back of the book to illustrate how you can teach this idea to your children).

With these ideas in mind, we started with our 16-year-old. We asked ourselves: what are Joshua's social, physical, intellectual, emotional, and spiritual needs at this point in his life? That is, what does he need to know, feel, and do, to be a balanced, healthy teenager and to eventually become a happy, healthy, productive adult? After discussing our teenager, we talked about Jordan's (our 9-year-old) needs. Once again, these discussions about needs are the first step required to complete The FTP.

Step 2 of the FTP calls for prioritizing this list of training needs and selecting those areas you will emphasize over a specific time period. Your effectiveness as a teacher will be greatly enhanced if you focus your efforts on one topic at a time. You cannot teach your children everything, so prioritize and focus your efforts on those things you deem to be most important and that are not likely to be taught by other institutions that your child is involved with, such as school or church.

Step 3 of the FTP step involves defining each of the things you plan to focus on. For example, if you plan to focus on the importance of regular exercise, clearly state what you want your child to know and do with regard to physical exercise, both as a child and as an adult. If you are trying to instill a work ethic, decide what you want your child to know and do in this area.

Step 4 is to develop a strategy to address each topic in your training efforts. Once again, if you plan to teach the importance of regular exercise, your strategy might be to take your children on a walk at a park at least four times per week. As your children grow older, you can explain the benefits of exercise, including: 1) improves concentration, 2) builds self-confidence,) increases creativity, 4) helps you relax, 5) reduces stress level, and 6) keeps weight within a desired range. When selecting a teaching strategy, remember that personal examples, for better or for worse, are powerful communicators. That is, a parent who does not exercise on a regular basis will no doubt have a more

difficult time convincing a child of the importance and benefits of exercise than a parent who participates in regular physical activity.

Life Skills: Education

<table>
<tr><td colspan="5" align="center">Table 6.
Lesson Ideas</td></tr>
<tr><th>Character</th><th>Family</th><th>Health</th><th>Safety</th><th>Social</th></tr>
<tr>
<td>work ethic
responsibility
attitude
honesty
perseverance
moderation
self-control
self-respect
respect for others
self-esteem
generosity</td>
<td>family support
parental standards
respect for parents
mate selection
marriage
parental roles
birth
separation and divorce
support services
love
traditions
genealogy/history
abuse</td>
<td>addictions
puberty/sexuality
alcohol and other drugs
tobacco
grooming
health care services
personal hygiene
consumer health
food labels
nutrition
physical fitness
stress
emotions</td>
<td>firearms
water safety
seatbelts
home safety
fire safety
accident prevention
violence
abuse
first aid skills
self-defense
electric storms
floods
tornadoes</td>
<td>dating
positive friends
pressure
interviewing for a job
etiquette
manners
assertiveness
friendship skills
respecting authority
discrimination
citizenship
sportsmanship
how to avoid gangs</td>
</tr>
<tr><th>Life Skills</th><th>Education</th><th>Spirituality</th><th>Boundaries</th><th>Finances</th></tr>
<tr>
<td>critical thinking
communication
conflict resolution
mediation
decision-making
planning
media literacy
motivation</td>
<td>studying for tests
homework
note-taking
time management
reading
college selection</td>
<td>prayer
religion
faith
voluntary service
golden rule
reverence
meditation
pornography
death</td>
<td>parental standards
parental discipline
personal standards
respecting authority</td>
<td>budgeting
checkbook
saving
investing
credit cards
charitable giving
fund raising
purchasing
negotiation</td>
</tr>
</table>

Both parents must participate honestly and openly (cooperate and work together) to ensure uniformity and consistency in the formulation and implementation of the plan. Children readily detect inconsistencies between parents and often exploit these divisions to their advantage.

If you are a single parent and rely heavily on another caregiver while working, you may want to involve this person in the planning process. At least inform this individual of what you are trying to accomplish in raising your children.

Whether you have a partner or are a single parent, it is important to acknowledge that others have an influence on your children during the course of their development. You may want to share your plan with close family members and friends who are exposed to your children on a regular basis. This will enable you to enlist their support in reinforcing those things you are teaching your children and will ensure that when they are around your children, they will do and say things that are in support of your own efforts.

As with developing a Family Management Plan, a side benefit that comes from working through the Family Teaching Plan steps with your spouse is found in the process required to arrive at a plan that you both agree on. This process requires good communication, self-disclosure, negotiation, and compromise. If this approach is taken seriously by investing the time and energy required to "get your act together," your teaching efforts will become more and more refined and effective over time. This refinement process will necessitate changes in the parenting plan as family circumstances change. Consider going on an annual retreat where you and your spouse can, without distractions, clarify and refine your plan. This retreat should be considered a time when the major strategies for parenting are "ironed out". The detail work on the plan should be an ongoing process whereby you meet together on a regularly scheduled basis (weekly or monthly) to discuss current issues and new ideas that may necessitate modifying the plan to meet the children's changing needs. Once again, these regularly scheduled meetings can help keep "help-mates" together on the particulars of their parenting strategy. For single parents, revisiting the plan on a regular basis can also be a time for reflection and refinement.

Once you have decided what principles you would like to teach your children, it is time to implement your plan of action. To find out whether or not you are having an impact, it is important you assess how your children are progressing. Yogi Berra once said, "You can observe a lot just by watching."

You can observe your children at any time. When you create an environment wherein children feel comfortable "being themselves," then you will have ample opportunity to discover how they are doing. In fact, parents who stay close to their children often get updates directly from their children. These updates can come in the form of discussion or, as is often the case when children get older, body language. Once again, however, parents must stay close to their children so they can pick up the subtle nuances in their behavior, so the child feels comfortable in sharing his or her feelings. One thing is certain: When parents use harsh discipline and chronic criticism when things are not just right, the child learns not to communicate unless things are going well. And, in turn, the parents are often uninformed until it is too late to help a child through a difficult spot, and then serious remedial action is required. For obvious reasons, this is especially poignant when a child commits suicide.

Table 7. Progress Tracker			
[1]Knowledge Questions	[2]Need?	[3]Behavior Questions	[4]Need?
Respect			
Honesty			
Responsibility			
Self-control			
Work			
Service			
Success			
Exercise			
Diet			

1. Things you want your child to know.
2. Discrepancy between what child knows and what he or she should know. Once you have identified a need, it is useful to find out why the need exists (i.e., the cause). If you know the cause(s) or why the child does not know or do what he or she should, then you can more readily come up with a solution(s) that addresses what is contributing to the need.
3. Things you would like the child to do.
4. Discrepancy between what the child does and what you would like the child to do.

Note: Many would argue that it is not the parent's role to try to shape the behaviors of their children, and that the role of a parent begins and ends with transmitting information. This is a nice idea, but it is not practical. When a child acts out or is not fulfilling designated assignments, a benevolent parent will provide appropriate consequences that are designed to shape the child's behavior in the best interest of the child. For example, if a small child screams incessantly, it may be appropriate to place the child in time-out. Or if a teenager is caught and arrested for DWI, it may be in the young person's best interest for you to withhold the car keys.

Table 7: Progress Tracker

Step 5 on the FTP is designed to help with the process of following up on your children's progress. It requires transferring what you plan to focus on during a specified time period onto the Progress Tracker displayed in Table 7.

As you will see, the Progress Tracker has four columns. Column 1 provides a space for you to list those things you want your children to know. Column 2 is for checking off when your children do not know something you want them to know. Column 3 provides space to list things you want your children to do. Lastly, in column 4 you designate a deficiency in a desired behavior. The form should only include those things you will focus on during a given period of time.

Remember, you cannot teach your children everything at once. Therefore, focus on those things most relevant to their personal needs, ages, and circumstances.

Because there is so much to teach, parents often do not know where to begin. A good starting point is to focus on meeting the informational and behavioral needs of your children. As you identify and note discrepancies between what behaviors you want to see in your children (as specified on the Progress Tracker) and what you actually observe, you have identified a need (the check marks you place in columns 2 or 4). Focus your efforts on meeting these needs. As one individual put it, "When we deal with generalities we rarely succeed; when we deal in specifics we rarely fail."

The process just described may seem time-consuming and burdensome. It is both. But, as I keep repeating, parenting is both time consuming and burdensome.

The alternative, however, is parenting without clear direction. The consequence of not taking the time and making the effort to "decide" where you are going is illustrated in the following Aesop's fable, The Man, the Boy and the Donkey (Æsop. Sixth century B.C.) Fables. The Harvard Classics. 1909–14):

A MAN and his son were once going with their Donkey to market. As they were walking along by its side a countryman passed them and said: "You fools, what is a Donkey for but to ride upon?"

So the Man put the Boy on the Donkey and they went on their way. But soon they passed a group of men, one of whom said: "See that lazy youngster, he lets his father walk while he rides."

So the Man ordered his Boy to get off, and got on himself. But they hadn't gone far when they passed two women, one of whom said to the other: "Shame on that lazy lout to let his poor little son trudge along."

Well, the Man didn't know what to do, but at last he took his Boy up before him on the Donkey. By this time they had come to the town, and the passers-by began to jeer and point at them. The Man stopped and asked what they were scoffing at. The men said: "Aren't you ashamed of yourself for overloading that poor Donkey of yours — you and your hulking son?"

The Man and Boy got off and tried to think what to do. They thought and they thought, till at last they cut down a pole, tied the Donkey's feet to it, and raised the pole and the Donkey to their shoulders. They went along amid the laughter of all who met them till they came to Market Bridge, when the Donkey, getting one of his feet loose, kicked out and caused the Boy to drop his end of the pole. In the struggle the Donkey fell over the bridge, and his fore-feet being tied together he was drowned.

"That will teach you," said an old man who had followed them: "You will not succeed if you have no plan."

The worst-case scenarios of parenting without forethought or direction can be devastating. The examples of the problems that occur in homes where youth are not given clear direction are endless. Planning takes time and is worth every minute invested.

26

TEACHING METHODS

In most cases, the way you teach—your teaching method—is as important as what you teach. This chapter presents a number of different teaching methods and a description of each method. Teaching methods are those learning activities used to communicate what you want your children to know and do about a particular subject or behavior. When planning a lesson, you will select one or more of these methods to accomplish the purposes of your lesson. The methods I describe here include 1) discussion, 2) question and answer, 3) computerized learning, 4) storytelling, 5) media-oriented, 6) visualization, 7) discovery or problem-solving, 8) lecture, 9) directed independent learning, 10) family outing, 11) demonstration, 12) role-playing and dramatization, 13) modeling, and 14) mixed methods. No, For Lord's sake, you don't need to learn or use them all. But do read on and when you find one or two that will work for your children, then study those and plan to use them. One or two…I mean it… don't overburden!

One more note before we get too deep into teaching methods. If you already know how your children learn best, then use the methods that complement their strengths. I have an associate who has three boys. Two are book learners and one is a kinesthetic learner. Thus, methods that use books work for two of them, but family outings and hands-on, "show me", methods, like the demonstration, work well for the third.

Discussion Method: This method is effective for developing respect for the ideas and opinions of others. When applying this method, you should do a considerable amount of planning to ensure the discussion does not get out of control. You should also designate a moderator. You can use this method when leading a discussion about what is the best way to overcome a particular problem the family is experiencing.

For example, if the children are not performing their assigned chores as they should, you could hold a council to review what tasks need to be done to maintain the house. You could allow the children to express their opinions about the best ways to get all these things done. Because this method allows everyone to contribute ideas, there is often more "buy-in." If the children's ideas are adopted, they are more likely to help implement their ideas.

Question and Answer Method: This method is much like the discussion method and can either be child- or parent-centered. If it is child-centered, the parents encourage the child to ask questions about a particular topic to gain more information. For example, the child could be encouraged to ask you about your childhood, such as what was hard about growing up, what was fun, what were some of the good things that happened to you, or how you overcame your problems.

If this method is parent-centered, the parents can ask questions to generate a discussion on a particular topic. For example, you can ask children a series of questions about their favorite foods, their favorite activities, their favorite people, problems that give them the most difficulty, problems that kids their age are facing, their most important goals, their most significant fears, and so on.

Whether child- or parent-centered, when first applying this method it is best to give everyone advance notice so all family members have time to prepare questions and think about the issue. The back-and-forth that occurs using this method is especially helpful in teaching good two-way communication skills. It is also a good method for obtaining both positive and negative feedback that can help create mutual understanding.

This method is an ideal way for you, as a parent, to informally transmit your personal values. The answers you give in response to your children's questions will be couched in your personal belief system, which will, in most cases, become your children's belief system until they are old enough to establish their own. Through this method, you can model appropriate ways of asking and answering questions.

Ask questions that stimulate thinking and encourage your children to respond. Questions can be asked that direct your children to search for information, think about what they have found, and apply the information to their personal lives.

Computerized Learning Method: There are a number of computer programs on the market that are designed to teach children a variety of lessons: math, reading comprehension, spelling, typing, anatomy and physiology, foreign languages, and so on. If you purchase and become familiar with these games, they can be used to help augment your child's learning at school and foster interaction between you and your child at home.

In addition, there are a number of reference programs you can suggest to your child when you want him or her to develop independent learning skills. I often tell my children when they are seeking information they can find answers to most of their questions on the World Wide Web. Simply assign your child to research a particular topic and then report back to the family on what he or she finds. This is with the understanding that children's activity on the web should be monitored and they should be taught about Internet safety (such as not giving out personal information).

Storytelling Method: This technique can be used to teach lessons in an entertaining manner. As long as the story is relevant to the child and captures the child's interest, it is likely that he or she will listen and learn from the story. This is particularly true if you prepare your children to listen for certain points you want them to gain from the story and then talk about these points afterwards.

Media-Oriented Method: Using media to convey information can add variety to your lesson and stimulate learning. Short videos, TV programs, photographs, music, video, and pictures can all be used to present a main message or to enhance messages conveyed by other methods. We have numerous videos that we use to reinforce lessons about manners, being concerned about the welfare of others, and so on. We have also purchased a number of CDs/programs that tell stories about famous individuals throughout history who displayed character traits we want our children to incorporate into their own lives. My wife makes it a point to watch certain TV programs (e.g., the Gilmore Girls, Glee, Mom) with our youngest daughter. During the programs, she will often push pause and discuss a scene and how it applies to our daughter's present or future life.

Mental Rehearsal and Visualization: This method requires those who use it to close their eyes and imagine something. This technique is often used when teaching people to relax. It can also be used to help people change the way they think about the things they experience. For example, if a person or a situation in your daily life causes stress-inducing thoughts, you can attempt to change the way you think of the situation or person (cognitive restructuring) by visualizing something positive about the situation —or by visualizing another situation or person altogether. You can even start singing a song or repeating a favorite quote to help you calm down. We know a person who begins silently reciting a verse in the Bible when he gets anxious (Proverbs, Chapter 3, verse 5). I will describe this approach is more detail below.

Discovery or Problem-Solving Method: This approach to teaching is effective with all ages. It entails setting up a problem your children are asked to solve. For example, present your teenager with a problem that many families commonly deal with, such as finances. Each child could be given a set amount of play money and told to practice budgeting their expenses for one month. Then provide your children with a variety of things they can choose to spend their money on: fun things, or things like bills and car payments. Once they have "spent" their money, if they chose to purchase non-necessities before or instead of paying bills, you can point out the consequences of their decisions (such as no lights, telephone, food, or air-conditioning, depending on what they neglected to pay).

More interestingly, have each child, (who is old enough to grasp the concept) actually be in charge of handling the family's finances for a month. This means going along to make a bank deposit of income, or electronically, and issuing all the checks after reviewing the bills (or again, doing them electronically). It will be an amazing eye opener for older children to see the mortgage, the taxes deducted from paychecks, the car payments, and the like. This type of problem-solving activity can help your children understand why they must be careful about how much they spend and on what. Assuming you are also saving, it will show how you save and for what purposes, trips, retirement, etc.

Lecture Method: This method usually involves standing or sitting in front of your children and imparting specific information. For example, you may have decided that you want your children to do certain chores, so you review the chore list to make each child aware of his or her assignments. Or you may explain a certain safety hazard and what each person should do to avoid the hazard.

The advantage of this method is that a great deal of information can be imparted. The disadvantage is that it is difficult to hold your children's attention if you use this method too liberally, particularly with young children, who have very short attention spans. In fact, lecturing should rarely be used with pre-teens. Even teenagers, who tend to be accustomed to the highly stimulating images and messages presented through the media and popular music, often become bored when information is presented in a lecture format. Hence, the lecture method should be used sparingly and/or briefly.

Directed Independent Learning Method: This is an important method for teaching children to take the initiative and the responsibility to learn on their own. For example, you can assign a child to find a book on a particular topic, read the book, and report back to the family on what he or she has learned. Another example is to encourage children to read the newspaper, or a source on the Internet that would have articles on your topic, and report back on a news event that captured their interest. You can then ask your children to find other sources on the same topic and make additional reports as more information about the event becomes available. This approach teaches young people how to probe deeper into the events that interest them. Initially, you should both structure and provide direction in this process until your children understand how to proceed on their own. For example, when you assign a particular topic you can also provide ideas about where to get information, how to summarize it, and how to present it in a concise and interesting manner.

Family Outing Method: Taking your children to a museum, farm, zoo, factory, hospital, court, or state park is a method of teaching that, in a school setting, is often referred to as a field trip. Family outings can help broaden your child's contacts in your community and provide them with a broader base of experience upon which to make decisions and interpret the world around them. For example, if you take your teenager to visit children in a pediatric oncology ward at a local hospital, your teen will gain a greater appreciation of health and the difficulties others must learn to cope with. This type of experience can help reinforce knowledge of compassion, courage, disease, health services, and so on. These outings should be well-planned so children are prepared for the experience and are looking for certain things you want them to learn.

Demonstration Method: Demonstration is a highly effective method, particularly if you are good at what you demonstrate. In fact, studies have shown that children often learn better from demonstrations than they do from verbal communication, especially when learning a skill. For example, if you want your child to clean a bathroom or mow the lawn, it is much better to work with him or her a few times and show what you expect than to simply say, "mow the lawn." Do not expect children to automatically absorb things you often take for granted. Do not be a "gotcha" parent who tells kids to do something and then gets upset when they do not do it exactly as you told them. It is hard to visualize complex behavior. In short, demonstrate what you want done as often as possible.

Role-playing and Dramatization Method: Children of all ages love dramatization and role-playing. This method involves writing or informally explaining a script that you ask your children to act out. You can also ask them to ad-lib a situation using their own creativity and imagination. For example, if you want to teach your children the skills required to resist peer pressure to smoke or drink, you can have them take turns tempting and resisting temptation.

This method goes along with demonstration. Once you demonstrate a behavior or skill, you can ask your children to role-play the skill to determine whether or not they have mastered the technique. You can, for example, demonstrate how you want your children to talk to one another—in soft, respectful tones—and then have them role-play what you have demonstrated.

Modeling Method: Perhaps the most effective technique of all, in terms of transmitting ideas about living, is role-modeling. For the most part, what your kids observe in your attitudes and actions is what you will eventually observe in their own attitudes and behaviors. They have the unique ability to see past your words. Modeling serves to teach and reinforce the messages you want to teach. This is why it is so important that you strive to become the person you want each of your children to become.

Mixed Methods: I like to use a variety of methods whenever I teach lessons. Just as a good cook uses a variety of main and side dishes to prepare a good meal, my wife and I have found that using a variety of methods ensures a much better lesson. Never "serve too much" of the same thing, or your children will tire of it and their learning will be inhibited. A very simple example of how we have used multiple methods is when we attempted to teach good table manners. We first explained the importance of using good table manners. We then demonstrated what we meant by displaying these same manners.

We have incorporated a variety of methods in the sample lesson plans provided at the end of this section. You should also try using a variety of methods when you prepare your own plans. As you become more experienced with the various methods, you will discover what we have: Some methods will work better with your family than others, and different methods are more effective with different age groups. When our children were very young, we told stories, sang songs, and played games. Now that we have older children, we have more guided discussions prompted by issues we think are relevant to the needs of each child.

27

DEVELOPMENTAL CONSIDERATIONS IN TEACHING

The lessons you prepare should be conducive to the age (developmental levels) and interest levels of the children. Although there are no set rules about what should be taught at the various developmental levels, there is agreement among most psychologists that children develop logical thinking in a more or less orderly sequence. This means before a child can master a higher-level concept, he or she must master a lower one. When teaching very young children, the concepts you teach should be very basic. These basic ideas provide a necessary foundation for the more advanced concepts that will follow. That is, build the foundation of your child's "house of knowledge" before you put on the roof. Furthermore, when preparing lessons for young children, you should realize they have short attention spans, they enjoy hands-on activities (play) more than talking, and they need very clear instructions. Therefore, lessons presented to youngsters should be brief and to the point and should involve some hands-on learning opportunities, even games that are adapted to the age of each child.

Perhaps the most important consideration here is personal relevance. Children of all ages are typically turned off by information that does not relate to them personally. Hence, when preparing a lesson, do what you can to present the main ideas in a context that is relevant to the age and developmental stage of the children. If you are planning to teach your teenage children about the negative effects of smoking cigarettes, rather than focusing on long-term consequences, such as lung cancer and emphysema, talk about the short-term negative effects of smoking, such as bad breath and social disapproval. A recent public service announcement used this approach with kids by relating such messages as, "When you kiss a smoker, it is like kissing an ashtray." Obviously, this message appeals to the immediate needs of teenagers, such as getting a date and being socially acceptable to their peers. A poster designed to prevent smoking among teenagers showed a box of rat poison alongside a cigarette and asked, "Did you know the same thing that is in rat poison is in cigarettes?" Once again, the message is simple but clear and relevant and uses a dramatic parallel to make a point, creating a higher-level cognitive message that teenagers can appreciate.

28

PSYCHOLOGICAL CONSIDERATIONS IN TEACHING

UNDERSTANDING AND APPLYING SOME BASIC PSYCHOLOGICAL principles when you are preparing a lesson can increase the likelihood that your children will adopt the attitudes and actions you believe are in their best interest. To this end, I endorse eight psychological conditions that leading social psychologists agree should exist if one expects an individual to adopt recommended attitudes or actions. In the context of parenting, this means that if you can create certain conditions around behaviors you want your children to adopt, then it will be much more likely for them to adopt these behaviors. There actually is a science to parenting that can be applied to ensure better results. The eight conditions that, according to Dr. Marty Fishbein and his colleagues (1991), you should strive to create are displayed in Table 8.

Table 8.
Psychological Conditions Important to Behavioral Compliance

To increase the likelihood that your child will adopt or abstain from a certain behavior (homework, regular exercise, not using drugs, or delaying sex until marriage) he or she—

1. **MUST** form a strong positive intention (or make a commitment) to do what you recommend.
2. **MUST** have the skill(s) necessary to do what you recommend.
3. **MUST** have few environmental constraints that prevent him or her from doing what you recommend.
4. **SHOULD** believe that the advantages of doing what you recommend outweigh the disadvantages.
5. **SHOULD** perceive that there is more social pressure to do what you recommend than not to do it.
6. **SHOULD** believe what you recommend is consistent with his or her self-image and does not violate his or her personal standards.
7. **SHOULD** have a positive reinforcement for doing what you recommend he or she do.
8. **SHOULD** believe (have confidence) he or she can do what you recommend.

Table 8: Psychological Conditions Important to Behavioral Compliance

The first three conditions shown in Table 8, (i.e., intention, ability, and environmental constraints) are considered "necessary and sufficient" for inducing your child to behave in a certain way. In other words, for a given behavior to occur, your child must 1) have a strong positive commitment or intention to perform the behavior, 2) have the skills required to implement the behavior, and 3) live in an environment that is conducive to the behavior's occurrence. For example, if he or she is committed to delay sex until marriage; has the skills required to resist peer pressure to engage in sex; and has a supportive home, school, peer, and/or church environment, it is very likely that he or she will delay the onset of sexual activity.

The remaining five conditions, see the SHOULDS in Table 8, are viewed as influencing the strength or intensity and direction of [your child's] intention to do what you want them to do. In keeping with the example of delaying sexual activity, your child will be more likely to form a strong intention to delay sex if (4) he or she believes that this behavioral choice will result in more positive (e.g., freedom from guilt, better health) than negative (e.g., unwanted pregnancy or disease) outcomes; (5) he or she perceives more social pressure to delay sex than to engage in it; (6) he or she perceives that delaying the onset of sexual activity is consistent with his or her self-image and does not violate his or her personal or family standards; (7) his or her emotional reaction to delaying sex is positively reinforced; and 8) he or she is confident that he or she can delay sexual activity.

These same eight conditions apply to many (if not all) behaviors you want your children to adopt. For example, if you are striving to get your child to study on a regular basis, you should work to ensure your child 1) makes a strong positive commitment to study every night, 2) has adequate study skills, 3) has a designated area to study without interruptions, 4) believes the choice to study will result in more positive (e.g., good grades, parental approval, less stress, success in life) than negative (e.g., placed on restriction by parents, no driver's license, not admitted to a preferred college) outcomes, 5) perceives more social pressure to study than to not study, 6) perceives that studying is consistent with his or her self-image and does not violate his or her personal standards, (7) has an emotional reaction to studying that has been positively reinforced, and 8) has confidence he or she can indeed study. To further help you apply these principles, I have incorporated them into the sample lessons at the end of the book.

29

CREATING AN ENVIRONMENT FOR LEARNING

ALTHOUGH IT IS NOT GOOD TO BE OVERLY RIGID ABOUT THE environment, it is necessary to establish and maintain an appropriate setting for learning. This can be accomplished by creating a congenial and informal atmosphere in which communication can flow openly.

Set standards for appropriate conduct during your family meetings and sensitively encourage everyone to adhere to these standards. Remember, however, that the reason for bringing your family together is more about learning to talk and enjoy being together as a family than about starting and finishing a lesson. If you are not flexible and loving in your approach to these meetings, your children will dread them instead.

If you can see that a meeting is not going as planned because someone is irritable or has a need that is different from what you originally planned, do not hesitate to modify, delete, add insights or materials, or change course altogether to meet the needs of those you are teaching. I have been prepared to teach what I thought was an important lesson only to find our children were exhausted and could not devote the necessary attention to learn the concept. With experience, I have learned to always have a back-up plan for times like these. I have made the decision to rent a video, go out for ice cream, play a game, or just talk. However, I always try to do something to preserve the habit of meeting together on a set night. If you do not do this, you run the risk of losing the habit.

30

PREPARING A LESSON PLAN

To help you prepare to teach, I have provided you with guidance on how to develop a lesson plan, as shown in Table 9. In addition, I have provided you with 22 sample lesson plans that relate to one or more of the topic areas I have just described. Many of the sample lessons are quite extensive, so you may spend more than one session on each lesson.

Please note: Of the 22 plans, only a few are being presented in this part of the book (1-9). The rest, if you decide to go deeper into the Lesson concept, are in the Appendix. In this way, for those of you interested in trying this concept out, the most important ones appear here, and the rest, equally important to most of you, will be found in the Appendix. You decide which to teach and how deep you believe you can dive with your family.

If the topic is especially important for your family, you may even want to spend an entire month focusing on that topic, but, at the risk of losing the family's interest, consider doing a week, then some other topic/s, and coming back two or three weeks later. For example, the first lesson I suggest you teach is the lesson on creating and maintaining a functional family. This lesson provides a foundation for what you are trying to accomplish with your family.

Because the lesson is quite extensive, it should be subdivided, according to your needs, into many different, yet related lessons.

For those of you not so deep into this concept yet, do it for the one week. Then, if there is material you have missed, or if the family expresses interest in pursuing this topic, feel free to come back to it for another week in a month or so. Make sure to take 10 or 15 minutes to review the first week's work, and then continue. In this way, you won't be doing four weeks in a row that will eventually remove the interest level from even the most curious among us.

Another lesson that is likely to take up more than one session is resisting peer pressure. As is noted in our sample lesson plan on this topic, you could easily extend this lesson by incorporating a directed independent learning experience that could last for two or more weeks. But, again, plan to do those additional weeks after reviewing some other lessons. Who knows, the family may want to get attached to another topic and that attachment will help to create the overall interest level that keeps everyone engaged week after week.

To reiterate, please do not feel like once you start discussing a particular lesson, you must finish it in one session or you must continue on with the lesson if your children want to talk about something else. If you doggedly stick to a lesson, your family sessions may begin to feel a lot like "school" *in a bad way*.

The main point of your teaching activity is to set aside time to discuss issues important to you and your children. It is a time everyone should enjoy—a time when everyone gets to participate freely.

You should also be aware if you tend to dominate the discussions and/or always choose the lessons, your children may feel inhibited to talk. They will simply "shut down" in spite of their natural tendency to want to talk about or even challenge your ideas. I have learned that a child "convinced against his will is of the same opinion still." (Dale Carnegie, How to Win Friends and Influence People).

We have agreed when we sit down and talk as a family on a

weekly basis (even though we often veer away from what we plan to discuss), we achieve some measure of success. In fact, sometimes instead of having a lesson we play a game, eat a snack, and just talk. Sometimes we do not even finish the game. This is to say children tend to be more engaged when they know their needs and preferences are more important than a lesson schedule.

Table 9.
How to Develop a Lesson Plan

TOPIC OF THE LESSON_____

WHAT I WANT THEM TO KNOW
Record the knowledge objectives of the lesson plan. These statements should be brief and to the point. For example, if you want your child to know what the family rules are, state, "By the end of this lesson, my child will know what the family rules are."

WHAT I WANT THEM TO DO
Record the behavioral objectives of the lesson. That is, what you want your child to do as a result of this lesson. For example, "As a result of this lesson, my child will be able to properly vacuum the carpet in the living room," or "My child will be able to take a phone message that is complete and correct."

WHAT I PLAN TO TEACH (What it is, why it's important, what they should know about it)
Record all the points you want to make during the lesson. This information should correspond with what is stated in your knowledge and behavioral objectives. For instance, if your knowledge objective is "to know what the family curfew is on Friday nights" and the behavioral objective is "to come in from a date before curfew" then, in this section, you will need to be explicit about what the curfew is and provide some incentive for compliance.

HOW I PLAN TO TEACH IT (My Methods)
Record the teaching methods that you will use to teach the things you have specified in the previous section.

HOW I PLAN TO FIND OUT IF THEY KNOW AND DO WHAT I WANT THEM TO
Record your plan for following up to determine whether or not your lesson was effective. The *Progress Tracker* should be used for this purpose, in addition to observation and other appropriate means of determining whether or not your children/teenagers are on track.

HOW I PLAN TO REINFORCE WHAT I HAVE TAUGHT
Record your plans for reinforcing messages. Given that your children will likely be exposed to many messages that are contrary to what you teach them, reinforcing your message is crucial if you hope to have a lasting impact. Message reinforcement is like giving booster shots to ensure full immunity against diseases.

SAMPLE LESSON PLANS 1 THROUGH 9

As stated previously, I have provided you with a number of lesson plans. Some of these plans, however, are quite extensive and, in most instances, will take two or more sessions to teach.

Again, these are the most commonly asked for topics by both parents and children. There are an additional 15-20 plans in the Appendix in case your important topics aren't in this group.

SAMPLE LESSON PLAN #1
WE WANT TO HAVE A HIGHLY FUNCTIONAL FAMILY

WHAT I WANT THEM TO KNOW

- There are differences between functional and dysfunctional families.
- We, as your parents, want to have a highly functional family. There are things each of you can do to help us attain this goal.
- To have a functional family requires work on the part of every family member.

WHAT I WANT THEM TO DO

- Learn what it takes to have a functional family.
- Do their part to help our family be functional.

WHAT I PLAN TO TEACH

- We should be able to identify and to adopt positive characteristics of a highly functional family.

- Each family member can do to better to ensure that we have a functional family.

HOW I PLAN TO TEACH IT (MY METHODS)

- Ask family members to brainstorm the characteristics of a functional family.
- Ask them to brainstorm the characteristics of a dysfunctional family.
- Assign children to discuss a different characteristic of a functional family, for each session.
- Discuss a different functional characteristic, for each session, emphasizing what each person should do to incorporate these characteristics into his or her own life.
- Commit each child to work on one functional characteristic for each session.

HOW I PLAN TO FIND OUT IF THEY KNOW AND DO WHAT I WANT THEM TO

- Observe how well they adhere to the functional family character traits.
- Hold one-on-one interviews using the Progress Tracker to determine if children can recognize, and are adopting, these character traits.

HOW I PLAN TO REINFORCE WHAT I HAVE TAUGHT

- I will set a good example by living these traits.
- I will post functional family traits and refer to them often.
- When I observe children deviating from desired traits, I will remind them their actions are working against our goal to have a functional family.

SAMPLE LESSON PLAN #2
WE BELIEVE IN BEING HONEST

WHAT I WANT THEM TO KNOW

- You should be honest in all your dealings.
- Even though it can be hard at times, honesty has many benefits.
- Half-truths are lies.
- Lies have many negative consequences.
- When you betray a confidence, you are being dishonest.
- When you slack off at work, you are being dishonest.
- Learn to use discretions — Whether you approve or not, when Grandma makes a pie and it tastes awful, we all say it is fine so as not to hurt Grandma.

WHAT I WANT THEM TO DO

- Always tell the truth, regardless of the consequences.
- Always be fair and honest in all their dealings with other people.

WHAT I PLAN TO TEACH

- A person who is honest always tells the truth, does not tell half-truths or withhold important information when giving an account of a situation.
- Honesty is the basis of any good relationship. If people are honest, you can trust them. People respect honesty. They are suspicious of those who are not honest.
- Our family believes you should be honest in all your dealings—both in the big things and the little things. Even though it can be hard at times, honesty has many benefits. If you are honest with us, your parents, we will reward you with more freedom because we know you can handle it and you will tell us the truth if there is a problem.
- Lying has many negative consequences. Liars are dishonest. They cannot be trusted because when it is in their best interest they will lie, distort the truth by telling half-truths, and so on.
- When someone tells you a secret, you should keep it confidential. People who betray confidences are dishonest and lose the trust of others.

HOW I PLAN TO TEACH IT (MY METHODS)

- Ask how people feel about those who are honest.
- Ask how people feel about those who lie.
- Brainstorm ways that people can be dishonest (little and big ways).
- Discuss negative things that can result when a person is dishonest.
- Tell a story illustrating consequences of lying: "The Boy Who Cried Wolf."

HOW I PLAN TO FIND OUT IF THEY KNOW AND DO WHAT I WANT THEM TO

- Observe the honesty of each child.
- Hold one-on-one interviews using Progress Tracker to determine what children know about honesty and how honest they are.

HOW I PLAN TO REINFORCE WHAT I HAVE TAUGHT

- Set a good example of honesty.
- Post a sign that says, "Honesty is Always the Best Policy." Caveat: With all the signs and charts and plans posted somewhere in your house, make sure there is room left on the walls for the kids' artwork?
- Read quotes every day that demonstrate that honesty is a good thing.

Parents, it should be understood that very young children (aged 7 and younger) often say things that are not true because they have vivid imaginations and desire adventure and fun. They often mistake their imagination for what is real. In such cases, you should help them sort out what is true and what is not. Because young children are not fully capable of knowing the difference between right and wrong, they should not be punished for such statements. If you do punish them at this stage of their development for something as simple as making up a "tall tale," you will be curtailing their imagination and inhibiting their natural desire to communicate all the wonderful things they feel and think as they experience the world for the first time.

SAMPLE LESSON PLAN #3
WE BELIEVE IN MAKING AND SAVING MONEY

WHAT I WANT THEM TO KNOW

- There are many ways to make money. Both working and investing are at the top of our list. Work wages and savings are predictable. Investing involves risk. Savings and so it works for you when you are not working, even when you are sleeping.
- You should manage your money with a budget.
- You should try to avoid debt.
- You should learn about investing, if only the basics.
- You should give 10 percent of your money to a charitable cause.
- You should always save 10 percent of what you make.
- We cannot give you money every time you ask for it, or buy you something every time you want it.

WHAT I WANT THEM TO DO

- Acquire knowledge and develop skills that they can use to make money.

- Create a budget and manage their money accordingly.
- Pay 10 percent of their earnings to a charitable cause.
- Save 10 percent of their earnings.

WHAT I PLAN TO TEACH

- There are many ways to make money. The best way is to work for it. You can do certain chores around the house that we will pay you for; you can mow lawns and do other odd jobs for our neighbors; and when you are old enough, you can get a job.
- You should manage the rest of your money with a budget.
- You prepare a budget by listing all the things you want to buy or activities you want to participate in during a specified period of time (a week or a month) on the left side of a piece of paper. On the right side of the paper, list the costs of these items. Total the column on the right. Remember, if the total is more than you earn, you will need to sacrifice an item in the left column, reduce the amount you spend on it, or increase your income. Making and following a budget like this will help you prioritize your expenditures. If you live within your budget, you will never go into debt. When you are young, we will help you buy things. As you get older, you will need to buy things for yourself. When you get to that point, you will be your "own person". It is a great feeling to be able to take care of your own needs. In sum, the purpose of a budget is to wisely control your money.
- The reason we cannot give you money every time you ask for it, or buy you something every time you want it, is because we have a limited income and if we spend more than we make, we will go into debt.
- Debt is incurred when you borrow money to buy things you cannot afford to purchase for cash at that moment. It

is a bad thing in most cases because you must work for money that is already spent. It can be very discouraging to make money and give it to someone else without receiving anything in return.
- Debt can cause you a lot of stress. Avoid debt you can't afford to pay back. Only take on debt that enables you to move forward in life — car, house, business, etc.
- It is important to understand 'good debt' and 'bad debt'.
- It is good to have 'good debt' when it is time, and if done correctly.
- It is not good to have 'bad debt', primarily because it is expensive and unproductive.

HOW I PLAN TO TEACH MY IDEAS (MY METHODS)

- Ask for ideas about how to make money.
- Review our family standards for charitable giving and saving money.
- Explain the importance of a budget.
- Show them the family budget and explain how it works.
- Help each child develop his or her own budget.
- Explain the importance of staying out of debt. Demonstrate how debt works.
- Read a short book on how to save money.
- Watch a video on the basics for kids of investing.

HOW I PLAN TO FIND OUT IF THEY KNOW AND DO WHAT I WANT THEM TO

- Hold one-on-one interviews using the Progress Tracker to determine what the children know about making and saving money, charitable giving, and debt, and ask them whether or not they are doing what we have suggested they do regarding these matters.

- For example: Do you have a budget? Are you referring to your budget every time you get paid?

HOW I PLAN TO REINFORCE WHAT I HAVE TAUGHT

- Help each child open a savings account.
- Help them make deposits in their savings and give money to a charitable organization through the appropriate channels.
- Review the family budget at family council.
- Show them how we save money for a family vacation. When on vacation, remind children the vacation was made possible only because of planning and saving.

SAMPLE LESSON PLAN #4
WE BELIEVE IN SETTING GOALS

WHAT I WANT THEM TO KNOW

- Setting goals can help you accomplish things that you would not otherwise accomplish.
- Achieving goals can help improve your self-esteem.
- You must have action plans to achieve your goals.
- Goals should be specific.
- Goals should be written down.
- Goals should be realistic.
- Goals should be stated in terms of a specific time period.
- Goals should be directed toward accomplishing good things in your life.
- You should review your goals on a regular basis.
- There are short term goals and long terms goals.

WHAT I WANT THEM TO DO

- Write goals in their journal that describe what they want to accomplish this month, this year, and before they graduate from high school.

- Write what action steps they will need to take to accomplish each goal.
- Read their goals once a week and record progress. List any additional action steps they may need to take to accomplish their goals, and write down any new goals.

WHAT I PLAN TO TEACH

- Goals are written statements that explain what you want to obtain or accomplish within a certain period of time.
- Action plans are those specific things you plan to do to achieve your goals.
- Setting goals can help you accomplish things that you would not otherwise accomplish.
- Achieving goals can help improve the way you feel about yourself.
- Goals should be specific and written down. Goals should be realistic and be stated in terms of a specific time period. To ensure that your goals will lead you to accomplishing good things in life, you should regularly review your goals and adjust them, as needed.
- Write goals in your journal that describe what you want to accomplish this month, this year, and before you graduate from high school. Then write what action steps you will need to take to accomplish your goals.
- Review your goals once a week. At this time you should record progress toward your goals, list any additional action steps you may need to take to accomplish your goals, and write down any new goals.

HOW I PLAN TO TEACH IT (MY METHODS)

- Ask children what goals are and why goal-setting is important.

- Ask them if they have ever set goals and, if so, whether or not they achieved them.
- Ask them what must be done to achieve goals.
- As per above, explain what goals and action plans are, why they are important, and how to write them down.
- Tell a story, read a book, or show a video that depicts someone who benefited from setting goals.
- Show the children my goals and action plans. Tell them about some of the goals I have set and accomplished and what I had to do to achieve them.
- Use the following format to teach children how to write goals and action plans:
- What I Want To Accomplish/Obtain
- (My Goals)
- How I Plan To Accomplish/Obtain This
- (My Action Plans)
- Help each child write down a goal he or she can accomplish in the next week, along with the action plans required to reach the goal.
- Assign children to report on their goal at the next family meeting.
- Help each child write down a long-term goal and the action plans required to accomplish it.

HOW I PLAN TO FIND OUT IF THEY KNOW AND DO WHAT I WANT THEM TO

- Hold one-on-one interviews using the Progress Tracker to determine what they know about goal-setting and writing action plans and what they are doing to accomplish their goals.

HOW I PLAN TO REINFORCE WHAT I HAVE TAUGHT

- Set and report on my personal goals.
- Set family goals and write action plans.
- Review status of family goals in weekly family meeting.
- At the beginning of every year, hold a special family meeting to set our family goals for the year.

SAMPLE LESSON PLAN #5
RECOGNIZING AND MANAGING STRESS

WHAT I WANT THEM TO KNOW

- Stress is the strain we feel when things happen to us.
- It is important to understand stress so we can manage it.
- We can learn strategies to help us manage, and sometimes even avoid, stress.

WHAT I WANT THEM TO DO

- Learn to recognize stress.
- Learn to avoid unnecessary stress triggers.
- Learn to manage stress.
- Take actions that lessen the negative effects of stress.

WHAT I PLAN TO TEACH

- Stress is the strain we feel when negative or positive things happen to us.
- Some stress is unavoidable, like an increased workload at school, serious personal injury, changes in school or

living conditions, a flat tire on your bike or car, and/or the death of a pet, friend, or family member.
- Stress can be either beneficial or harmful, depending on how we prepare for and deal with it.
- A little stress can be good. For example, before we play an important game, take a test, participate in a recital, or act in a play, we may feel stress that helps us adapt to the situation by increasing our mental and physical alertness.
- Although moderate amounts of stress can be helpful, extreme amounts of stress can harm both our bodies and our minds. This is particularly true when we are under extreme stress for a sustained period of time. Under extreme stress, we can become overwhelmed, and our ability to perform even simple tasks can be compromised.
- We can take steps to avoid extreme stress. For example, we can fortify ourselves against stress by living balanced lives. People who exercise, eat good food, get adequate sleep, engage in spiritual activities, feel good about themselves, and so on, are better able to deal with stress. If you prepare yourself to accomplish your goals, you will more likely succeed and suffer less stress when the opportunities you desire present themselves.

- For example, if you want to be a famous singer and you never practice singing until a few days before you have an audition, you will feel a lot of stress and probably not perform at your best, which may prevent you from reaching your goal. If you do not study for a test until the night before, taking the test may be a very stressful experience. The stress connected with this test could have been avoided if you had studied for an hour each day rather than trying to cram the night before. If you hope to win a track meet and you do not practice, you will lack the confidence and stamina to do your best.

- Negative things that can cause stress include a poor diet, not being prepared for a test, getting yelled at by a parent or teacher, lacking confidence in your ability to do something you must do (like sing a solo), and irresponsible behavior in general.
- You can avoid stress to a great extent if you are/become a responsible and a self-disciplined person.

Some things you can do to manage stress include the following:

1. Better prepare for whatever task you find difficult,
2. Review your school subjects every night whether or not you have homework,
3. Be kind to others because others will likely treat you as you treat them,
4. Get up earlier so you are not rushed when getting ready for school,
5. Pray daily, asking for help when you need it,
6. Read books or watch movies about how to overcome or to manage stress,
7. Relax and talk positively when you feel stress,
8. Live a balanced life,
9. Keep a journal and record your frustrations or work out a plan to overcome them,
10. Do what you say you will do,
11. Tackle hard tasks first, then focus on less important tasks,
12. Do not over-commit yourself and, if you do, enlist the help of others to get everything done, and
13. Serve others.

HOW I PLAN TO TEACH IT (MY METHODS)

- Explain what stress is.
- Ask what causes stress.
- Ask what can be done prevent stress.

- Ask what can be done to manage stress.
- Have children list the things they can change in their lives.
- Present ideas on how to reduce stress and how to prevent the negative mental and physical effects of stress.
- Listen to a tape on how to relax.

HOW I PLAN TO FIND OUT IF THEY KNOW AND DO WHAT I WANT THEM TO

- Set a good personal example of how to reduce and manage stress.
- Hold one-on-one interviews using the Progress Tracker to determine what each child is doing to reduce and manage stress.

HOW I PLAN TO REINFORCE WHAT I HAVE TAUGHT

- Put up a poster that lists all the ways our family can avoid stress. Refer to the poster throughout the week.
- Compliment children when I observe them doing things that reduce stress.
- Watch a video that talks about how to relax.
- Listen to a CD about managing stress.
- Turn off television on Sundays and listen to relaxing music.

SAMPLE LESSON PLAN #6
HOW TO GET AND KEEP POSITIVE SELF-ESTEEM

WHAT I WANT THEM TO KNOW

- Some people think they are better than others. A person with a high self-esteem actually shows respect to other people rather than acting superior toward them.
- Many people think they are not as good as others when, in fact, each and every person is of great worth and deserves to be treated with respect.
- It is important that you have high self-esteem.
- You can do specific things to ensure that you gain and maintain high self-esteem.

WHAT I WANT THEM TO DO

- Strive to attain and maintain high self-esteem
- Love themselves

WHAT I PLAN TO TEACH

- Self-esteem is how good you feel about yourself.

- People who have high self-esteem feel good about themselves. They like themselves. They feel a sense of accomplishment in their lives. They recognize their talents and abilities and use them to improve their lives and the lives of others. They believe life is good in spite of the problems they must face. They do better in school and work and have more confidence in their personal abilities. They are typically more successful than those who do not have high self-esteem.
- When you are young, the way you feel about yourself has a lot to do with what other people have said to you. Parents and peers can either send positive or negative messages that help you create your perception of who you think you are and how good you are. Unfortunately, many people are exposed to a lot of bad messages from insensitive people, and they develop a low self-esteem. This is unfortunate, because everyone who has ever been born on this earth has worth and value. Therefore, everyone should and can learn to develop high self-esteem that can help him or her become happy and successful.
- As you strive to develop high self-esteem, always remember that you are a person of great worth, that you are unique, and that you have many things you can contribute to society (regardless of your circumstances). Also, learn to set realistic goals and then set a plan for reaching them. People who consistently accomplish goals in their lives have a tendency to feel better about themselves.
- Strive to say what you mean and mean what you say. That is, if you tell someone you will do something for him or her, then do it.
- Live a balanced life. If you eat right, exercise regularly, and get adequate rest, you will look better and feel better about yourself.

- When you talk to yourself (which we all do in our minds), say mostly good things. It is okay to be upset with yourself when you do not do what you know you should. However, at the same time, if you are upset with yourself, you should assure yourself that you will do better next time, and then think about ways of avoiding the same mistake. We are all "works in progress." No one is perfect. We all make mistakes. What is important is that we work on our weaknesses. If we do, we will eventually overcome them.
- Some threats to your self-esteem include hanging around people who always put you down and doing what others want you to do instead of doing what you feel is best.
- People who do things that go against their personal values can develop low self-esteem. To avoid this, you could keep a journal that lists how you feel about things that are important to you. Read it often to remind yourself of your goals and ideals. This will help you "watch yourself," so you can avoid doing things that will make you feel bad.
- This can also help you make decisions about what you should and should not do with your life. For example, if you believe it is wrong to be unkind to other people, but you are unkind to your family, then you will feel guilt and this can cause you to feel bad about yourself. Likewise, if you feel like people should not steal or lie but you steal or lie a lot, you will begin to feel bad about yourself. The point here is to watch yourself. If you start to do something and you get an "uh oh" feeling, do not repeat the bad behavior. Feelings of guilt and disappointment help you recognize what you are doing may not be right.
- You can learn to neutralize and process negative messages in a positive way; this is called cognitive restructuring. For example, if you really like playing the

guitar and someone overhears you practicing and makes the comment, "You're not that great," say to yourself, "Not yet." If someone says to you, "Gee, you're dumb," say to yourself, "Not when I study."
- To overcome bad feelings that result when you do things you should not, be determined to "bounce back" and do better the next time. If you have hurt someone, ask for forgiveness. Read your journal often as a constant reminder of what is important to you.
- Commit yourself to work on developing high self-esteem and avoiding those things that can make you feel bad about yourself.

HOW I PLAN TO TEACH IT (MY METHODS)

- Ask, "What is self-esteem?" After fielding a few responses, explain what it is.
- Ask family members to close their eyes and imagine (using the visualization method) that they are looking in the mirror. Ask them to think about how they feel about the person they see in the mirror. "Do you believe this is a nice person, a good person, a talented person, a friendly person? Do you like this person?"
- Ask everyone to write down something nice about everyone else in the family. Collect the lists and read the nice things aloud. Make the point that we can influence how others feel about themselves. Because of this, we should say things to support and encourage one another rather than say cutting and discouraging things.
- Ask, "What helps a person have high self-esteem?"
- Ask, "What makes a person feel bad about him or herself?"
- Role-play cognitive restructuring by having one person make a negative comment and the other explaining out

loud how he or she can restructure the comment to diffuse it.
- Ask what can be done to develop high self-esteem.
- Ask what can cause us to have low self-esteem.
- Explain the benefits of high self-esteem and the problems of low self-esteem.
- Ask for ideas about how they can overcome forces that diminish self-esteem.
- Explain what they can do to gain and maintain high self-esteem: set goals and reach goals, live in accordance with their values, be kind to others ("what goes around comes around"), serve others, etc.
- Explain how they can avoid or overcome things that can diminish their self-esteem.
- Have them list things that are important to them: kindness, helpfulness, exercise, getting good grades, playing the piano, getting along with other people. Explain that it is important to live in a way that is consistent with their values (those things that are important to them) to avoid having low self-esteem. Encourage them to place the things they have written in a journal and refer to them often.

HOW I PLAN TO FIND OUT IF THEY KNOW AND DO WHAT I WANT THEM TO

- Observe their attitude and behavior.
- Hold one-on-one interviews using the Progress Tracker to determine how they feel about themselves. Also determine whether or not they are consistently striving to improve their self-esteem, encourage positive self-esteem among others, and avoid things that can threaten their self-esteem.

HOW I PLAN TO REINFORCE WHAT I HAVE TAUGHT

- Post a sign that lists the nice things others say about each individual family member (add those things that were listed during the lesson activity).
- Ask family members to add to this sign as they think of or observe good things about other family members. (For example, Jordan is good on his roller blades, is very responsible about doing his chores, loves to help his mom and dad to work around the house, and does well in school.)

SAMPLE LESSON PLAN #7
DEVELOPING STRATEGIES TO RESIST PEER PRESSURE

WHAT I WANT THEM TO KNOW

- Peers will tempt you to do things that are wrong and even dangerous.
- You can learn to resist negative pressure.

WHAT I WANT THEM TO DO

- Practice and learn skills to resist negative pressure as a way to preserve family standards of ethics, health, and safety

WHAT I PLAN TO TEACH
   What it is:

- People your own age place pressure on you to do what they want you to do, regardless of the consequences.
- Sometimes your friends or someone your age will pressure you to do inappropriate things because they are having fun and want you to have fun. Oftentimes,

however, they pressure you because they do not feel good about something they are doing and want others to do the same thing, supposing that if many people do it, then "it's not so bad." Many times, the reason these individuals do not feel good about the things they are pressuring you to do is because they are insecure about something. For example, they may feel like it is dangerous or unlawful.
- Pressure tactics include begging you, calling you names, or rejecting you (saying they will not be your friend), if you will not do what they want you to do.
- Sometimes peer pressure makes you feel so bad you are tempted to give in and do what others want you to do, instead of what you want to do.

Why it is important:

- If you give in and do what others want you to do instead of what you think you should do, you become unhappy and confused.
- Therefore, you need to learn how to resist pressure to do things you do not really want to do.

There are a number of benefits to knowing how to resist pressure:

- If you learn to resist pressure to do what others want you to do, you will become a strong, self-directed, mature person. Mature people are those who make up their own mind about things and are not afraid to tell others how they feel. They are in control of their lives. They are cool.
- You should commit to not following along and doing things that can hurt you or that you may feel bad about later.
- These skills may help you avoid embarrassment.
- They can help you look intelligent.

- You will become a leader because people your age like other people who can stand up to pressure. They will want to follow you because they feel safe and supported in their decisions to not give in to pressure from others.

The disadvantages of not knowing how to resist pressure:

- You may not know what to say when others try to change your mind.
- If you do not learn these skills, you may give into pressure and become insecure.
- You may be embarrassed in front of friends when you could have avoided this and looked and sounded cool in your response.
- You become a follower, instead of a leader.

What you should do about it:

When people pressure you to do things you do not really want to do, you can:

1) say no and mean it,
2) use a comeback,
3) reverse the pressure, or
4) leave the place where you are being pressured.

SAY NO...

"Just say no" works when

1) you say no like you mean it, and
2) you say it with an assertive voice and body language.

COMEBACKS...

If the person who is pressuring you will not take no for an answer, do not give long explanations, just say something like, "Lighten up, dude/girl," "Read my lips, no," or "Which part of the word no don't you understand?" Other ways of saying no include, "Get off my back," "Get a life," "Don't you have anything better to do than bother me?" or "Get lost."

REVERSE THE PRESSURE COMEBACKS...

Ask these types of questions: "Why do you feel like you need to convince people to go along with you?" "What makes you think that your ideas are better than everyone else's?" "Do you think the world revolves around your thoughts?" "Why can't you just let other people do their own thing?" "Don't you think people that go around trying to get everyone else to do what they want are pushy?" "Why are you so pushy?" "Don't you think people who can have fun without drinking are more mature than those who have to drink to have a good time?" "Why do you have to drink to have fun? Are you addicted?" OR "Are you practicing your speech on me?

* EXIT THE SITUATION...

If all else fails, say something like, "I'm outta here," or "This isn't fun. I'm gone." Some kids get so embarrassed by pressure that they give into it and lose their lives. You can overcome embarrassment, but you cannot overcome the consequences of giving into something that can hurt or kill you. Don't die of embarrassment (literally).

Commitment:

Will you commit to learning and practicing comebacks?

HOW I PLAN TO TEACH IT

- Lecture to explain what negative peer pressure is and why it is important to learn to resist it.
- Ask children what kinds of peer pressure they have witnessed or experienced and get their ideas for resisting pressure.
- Demonstrate how to use comebacks.
- Role-play to allow children to practice comebacks.
- Use directed independent learning by assigning kids to

pretend some of their friends are pressuring them to use alcohol. Have them come up with their own comebacks and practice them for the next family meeting when you or others in the family will try to tempt them to give in.
- Post a sign in kitchen that lists the four things kids can do to resist peer pressure.

HOW I PLAN TO FIND OUT IF THEY KNOW AND DO WHAT I WANT THEM TO

- After teaching the entire lesson, have a follow-up session where each child will have a chance to practice resisting pressure to drink alcohol.
- Ask children to report on successes in resisting pressure.
- Hold one-on-one interviews using the Progress Tracker to determine how well children are resisting peer pressure.

HOW I PLAN TO REINFORCE WHAT I HAVE TAUGHT

- Make favorable (genuine) comments when the children practice their skills during the follow-up lesson.
- Post a sign in kitchen that lists the four ways of resisting pressure.

SAMPLE LESSON PLAN #8
PREVENTING ALCOHOL AND DRUG USE

WHAT I WANT THEM TO KNOW

- Using alcohol and other drugs can be harmful and result in many negative consequences.
- You do not need to use alcohol and other drugs to be happy or popular among your friends.

WHAT I WANT THEM TO DO

- Practice encouraging others not to drink alcohol or use other drugs.
- Practice resisting pressure to use alcohol and other drugs.

WHAT I PLAN TO TEACH

- Alcohol is a drug that alters the way you think and feel, as well as your ability to do things.
- Alcohol is called a depressant because it slows your body down.

- Using alcohol causes people to do things they would not otherwise do, like take dangerous risks.
- Abstaining from alcohol and other drugs can prevent many problems: health conditions, embarrassment, car accidents, unwanted sexual relations and pregnancy, and/or a bad reputation as a result of saying or doing things you would not normally do.
- Explain why people think they need alcohol when in fact they do not.

HOW I PLAN TO TEACH IT (MY METHODS)

- Lecture about alcohol and its negative physical effects.
- Ask children to add their ideas about some of these negative effects.
- Ask children why people drink if there are so many negative effects.
- Role-play resisting pressure to use alcohol with the following comeback strategies:

THE "I DON'T NEED TO DRINK ALCOHOL" COME-BACK STRATEGY...

When someone tries to get you to drink for any reason, say, "I don't need to drink." Consider the example below:

———

("Pressurer" says) "Take a drink."

(You say) "No!"

(Pressurer says) "Come on, it will help you have a good time."

(You say) "I don't NEED to drink to have a good time. Besides, alcohol is a depressant. I'm not here to get depressed. I came to have a good time."

(Pressurer says) "Come on, take a drink; it will help you loosen up."

(You say) "I don't NEED alcohol to loosen up."

(Pressurer says) "Come on, take a drink, it will help you feel better."

(You say) "I don't NEED a drug to feel better. I'll feel better when you're gone."

———

REVERSE THE PRESSURE

REVERSE THE PRESSURE by asking questions like the following:

"Why do you feel like you need to convince people to go along with what you want them to do?"

"What makes you think that your ideas are better than everyone else's?"

"Do you think the world revolves around your perspective?"

"Why can't you just let other people do their own thing?"

"Don't you think people who go around trying to get everyone else to do what they want are pushy?"

"Why are you so pushy?"

"Don't you think people who can have fun without drinking are more mature than those who have to drink to have a good time?"

"Why do you have to drink to have fun?" OR

"Are you addicted?"

Ask children to sign a contract or make a formal commitment not to drink.

HOW I PLAN TO FIND OUT IF THEY KNOW AND DO WHAT I WANT THEM TO

- Observe their role-playing to determine if they have adopted good comeback strategies.
- Ask them how they feel about drinking.
- Hold one-on-one interviews using the Progress Tracker to

determine if they feel confident in their ability to resist drugs and alcohol.

HOW I PLAN TO REINFORCE WHAT I HAVE TAUGHT

- Set a good example by not partaking in alcohol or illicit drugs.
- Point out the negative consequences of these substances whenever they become apparent in the media.

SAMPLE LESSON PLAN #9
DELAYING SEX UNTIL MARRIAGE

(Note: Some feel this is a religious decision, some a family decision, others have personal history to present, and still others may skip this 'lesson' altogether. I understand.)

WHAT I WANT THEM TO KNOW

- Your parents want you to delay sexual relations until you are married.
- If you commit yourselves and learn the skills needed to delay sex, you will be successful.
- Delaying sexual relations until marriage is consistent with our family values.
- You should realize the connection among thoughts, actions, and certain stimuli. For example, certain music and movies can provoke sexual thoughts that can tempt you to engage in sexual relations.
- Your parents want you to date, to get married, and to have babies, in that order.
- Sex is NOT bad in and of itself. But engaging in

premarital sex is a bad choice that is not consistent with our family values.
- Premarital sex has emotional and physical consequences.

WHAT I WANT THEM TO DO

- Take precautions against engaging in sex before marriage
- Refrain from sexual relations until married

WHAT I PLAN TO TEACH
What it is:

- Sexual relations include any kind of physical contact with another person that stimulates them sexually (i.e., passionate kissing, touching private parts, and sexual intercourse).
- If you refrain from sexual relations until marriage, you will have many advantages: you will have more time to 1) learn the relationship skills required to get along with others without sex, 2) test the love expressed by another person, 3) understand personal sexual motives, 4) learn to discern sexual motives and avoid sexual exploitation, 5) learn to recognize and avoid risky situations and safely escape from risky situations, 6) learn how to refute peer pressure, and 7) learn to control urges and to govern sexual thoughts and emotions.
- There are disadvantages of not knowing or doing. If you do engage in sexual relations before marriage, you run a greater risk of acquiring an STD (namely, HIV), becoming pregnant or causing a pregnancy, and/or performing poorly in school—or dropping out of school due to infection or pregnancy.

What you should do about it:

- Do not watch movies or listen to songs that tempt you to be sexual.
- Do not read pornography or visit pornography sites on the Internet.
- Do not entertain sexual thoughts.
- Do not start dating until you are at least 16, and then only date in groups.
- Do not date just one person until you are at least 18 years old.
- If you are having problems, talk to your parents or your religious leader.
- Formally commit (with a behavioral contract) to delay sexual relations until marriage.

Teach how you can actually achieve each of these do and do not goals. Sexuality is a strong emotion and requires an alternative outlet. Some parents will consider self-sexual attention, others will require abstention altogether.

HOW I PLAN TO TEACH IT (MY METHODS)

- Lecture briefly on what sex is and what our family values are concerning sexual activity.
- Ask children to give ideas about advantages of delaying and disadvantages of not waiting.
- Read list of advantages of delaying sex until marriage.
- Every child signs a contract to abstain and lists the advantages of abstaining.

HOW I PLAN TO FIND OUT IF THEY KNOW AND DO WHAT I WANT THEM TO

- Have a follow-up session to review abstinence contracts.

- Hold one-on-one interviews using the Progress Tracker to determine if children are facing any temptations with sexual intimacy.

HOW I PLAN TO POSITIVELY REINFORCE WHAT I HAVE TAUGHT

- Give a personal example such as explaining why you are committed to fidelity in your marriage.
- Share with the children videos and brochures that reinforce abstinence or alternatives as discussed above.
- Share testimonials from positive role models.

CONCLUSION AND SUMMARY

As I said at the outset of this book, to ensure the best outcomes, parenting should be approached systematically. To support this idea, I have provided you with ingredients to do the job. Specifically, I have given you guidance on how to create a vision, set goals, effectively manage your family, teach your children, and the tools required to do all of this in a way that will help you raise healthy humans with character.

Although the ideas I have supplied require an investment of time and energy, based on both my personal and professional experience, I know they will pay enormous dividends in the lives of your children. Moreover, if you set aside the time required to establish your parenting plan and do what I suggest to implement the plan (with your own modifications to fit your personal circumstances), you will accomplish much within the precious time you have to spend with your children. And accomplishing more with less means you are going to become a more efficient and effective parent.

APPENDIX:
MORE SAMPLE LESSON PLANS

SAMPLE LESSON PLAN #10
WE BELIEVE IN WATCHING OUR WORDS

WHAT I WANT THEM TO KNOW

- Words are vehicles that carry messages that can do good or harm.
- It is important to use language to help rather than to hurt people.
- You can learn to use words that will help you make and keep friends.
- Profanity and vulgarity are unacceptable. Do not use them at any time.
- What you say reflects on you and our family, for good or bad.
- You should use courteous words that convey respect when talking to adults.

WHAT I WANT THEM TO DO

- Monitor the words they use and how they use them
- Use words and phrases in a way that builds people up rather than tears them down

- Abstain from gossip ("he said, she said")

WHAT I PLAN TO TEACH

- Words are vehicles that convey messages. Some words convey very good messages, and some convey very bad messages that can make people angry.
- Using profanity and vulgarity are in violation of our family rules. Profanity is language that shows disrespect for religious things, like saying the name of the deity when you are upset. Many people are offended when these words are used.
- Vulgar words are crude or obscene words (cuss words) about body parts, body functions, or sex acts/organs that are characterized by lack of refinement, restraint, sensitivity, and good taste. Vulgar words convey ugly and aggressive messages and show disrespect for civil behavior. As with profanity, many people are offended by vulgarity, for they believe that the use of these words in public is a violation of their privacy. As one person put it, "The use of profanity or vulgarity represents a feeble mind trying to express itself forcefully (Mark Twain)."
- Many people who use profanity and vulgarity claim the right to do so under freedom of speech. However, when they use these terms in public, they diminish the freedom of those who are offended by them. Such words are like second-hand smoke; those who object to profanity but who are in the same room as people who use profane and vulgar language must hear this language when it is spoken.
- What you say reflects on you and our family. If what you say is good, it can reflect positively. If it is crude, vulgar, and profane, it will most definitely reflect negatively.
- Using the right kinds of words can protect you and others from violence. If you use words that make people

upset, it is possible that the offended person will use words that are upsetting to you. The result can be an angry confrontation, even a violent one. "Excuse me," "Pardon me," "I'm sorry," "I was wrong," "That was my fault," and other such phrases convey that you are a courteous person who respects others and takes responsibility for your mistakes. These phrases diffuse rather than provoke anger in others. As the Bible says, "A soft answer turns away wrath (Proverb 15:1)."

- Using phrases such as, "Yes, sir" and "Yes, ma'am," when communicating with an adult conveys that you respect the individual. Why? Because we respect all people.
- You should use courteous words that convey respect when talking to others. Courteous language can win you respect and popularity with others. If you do not understand something someone has said, you can respectfully respond with a phrase like, "Excuse me?" or "Pardon me?" These phrases convey both respect for the person you are speaking with, as well as the idea that you are an intelligent, alert individual. Refrain from using terms like "yea," "uh huh," "yep," "yis," "ya," and other slang words. Slang words convey the idea that you have a poor vocabulary, that you are not very intelligent, or that you are lazy. Speak clearly, especially when speaking with adults. When you mean yes or no, say yes or no, respectively. Always say what you mean and mean what you say. Carry through on your promises, even if it is a sacrifice. If you do what you say you will do, then you will gain the respect and admiration of others. Also, you will learn to watch what you promise to do. It is better to say no to a request than it is to say yes and not follow through.
- It is important that you use language to help rather than to hurt people.

- You should monitor your words to make sure that what you say is appropriate. "One of the first things a physician says to the patient is, 'Let me see your tongue.' A spiritual advisor might do the same" (N. Adams).
- Teach the negative consequences of gossip.

HOW I PLAN TO TEACH IT (MY METHODS)

- Ask children how they feel when other people use bad words.
- Ask them how they feel when they hear these words in public.
- Ask them why using these words is not appropriate. Ask, "What are some reasons that you can think of for not using these words?"
- Make all the points listed above in terms our children can understand.
- Ask, "Why shouldn't we support movies/TV where people use these words?"
- Play a game: Give each person a piece of paper and have him or her list words we use at our home that build up our family members. Then have them list all the words that are not appropriate because they tear down family members. Also, list those words that show disrespect for members of the family. Then bring out a nice jewelry box and put all the nice (or gem) words in the box. Then bring out a trash can and have everyone throw the bad words (the words that convey disrespect and bring people down) into the trash can. Label the words in the trash can "TRASH words," and make sure everyone sees us put them in the garbage. At this stage in the lesson, ask family members to try their best to not use TRASH or GARBAGE words because they do not belong in our house.

- Make a sign that says, "TRASH words don't belong in our house."

HOW I PLAN TO FIND OUT IF THEY KNOW AND DO WHAT I WANT THEM TO

- Observe how my children speak to their parents, to each other, and to their friends. Ask their friends (in a delicate way) what kind of language my child uses when he or she is not at home.
- Hold one-on-one interviews using the Progress Tracker to determine what they know and do about our family's language standards.
- Post a sign that says, "TRASH WORDS don't belong in our house."

HOW I PLAN TO REINFORCE WHAT I HAVE TAUGHT

- Stop and courteously remind the child when he or she uses inappropriate language.
- Use appropriate language instead of profane, vulgar, or crude language in my personal life.
- Avoid using slang (Use discretion here. Sometimes we use slang in fun, and teenagers have their own language that they use among themselves for fun).
- Encourage children to refrain from TV, videos, or music where vulgar and profane language is used.
- Every time a child uses an inappropriate word, have him or her write it on a piece of paper and throw it in the trash. Make the point that such words do not belong in our house.

SAMPLE LESSON PLAN #11
WE BELIEVE IN BEING GRATEFUL

WHAT I WANT THEM TO KNOW

- It is important to be grateful for the things that you receive in life.
- You should express your gratitude often.
- Expressing gratitude will make you and others feel better.
- Expressing gratitude has many advantages.
- There are many ways you can express and demonstrate gratitude.

WHAT I WANT THEM TO DO

- Express gratitude for things that others do for them
- Express gratitude for the things they enjoy in life
- Display a grateful attitude

WHAT I PLAN TO TEACH

- Gratitude is a feeling of thankful appreciation for favors/benefits received.
- Expressing gratitude is something that our family values.
- It is important to feel and express gratitude for the things you have and the things you will receive in the future.
- It is important to express gratitude, even when things are not going well. People who are grateful are much happier than those who are not.
- We have many things we take for granted that we should be grateful for. These include (list all things the family has that can be considered blessings).
- Happiness is not getting more but being grateful for the things you already have in life. When we are not grateful, we cannot enjoy the things we have. Do not put off being grateful until you get the next thing you want, because shortly after you get that thing, you will want something else—which means that you will always be putting off being grateful.
- There are many advantages to consistently expressing gratitude and having a grateful attitude. People like doing nice things for you if you show appreciation and express gratitude for the things that you receive. When you express gratitude on a regular basis, it reminds you of the good things in your life. People who express gratitude become optimistic about life because they see it from the bright side.
- There are many ways to express gratitude. These include saying "thanks," writing a thank you note, doing something nice for someone who has done something nice for you, helping and serving others, doing the dishes after a good meal, and so on.

HOW I PLAN TO TEACH IT (MY METHODS)

- List things some other people do not have that we enjoy,

such as sight, hearing, health, a home, a job, friends, and each other.
- Ask them what things they are grateful for.
- Ask them to name some of the people who made it possible for them to have these things in their life. Ask them for ideas about how they can express gratitude for these things.
- Make the points listed above.
- Show a video that portrays a character with a grateful attitude.
- Read a book about a character with a grateful attitude.
- Read quotes that support these principles about gratitude.

HOW I PLAN TO FIND OUT IF THEY KNOW AND DO WHAT I WANT THEM TO

- Hold one-on-one interviews using the Progress Tracker to determine what the children think and do about gratitude.
- Observe their attitudes and behaviors and offer compliments or gentle reminders, as needed.

HOW I PLAN TO REINFORCE WHAT I HAVE TAUGHT

- Model a grateful attitude by expressing appreciation for my blessings daily.
- Read a quote every evening that pertains to some aspect of gratitude.

SAMPLE LESSON PLAN #12
DEVELOPING AND MAINTAINING SPIRITUALITY

WHAT I WANT THEM TO KNOW

- It is important to develop yourself spiritually, have faith in God/Higher Power, and earnestly strive to do His will in your life.
- There are many things you can do to become a more spiritual person.
- The scriptures provide guidance that you can use as a standard to judge your thoughts and actions.
- There are many benefits to living in accordance with what is outlined in the scriptures.
- There are many disadvantages to not living according to these guidelines.

WHAT I WANT THEM TO DO

- Pray and meditate every morning and every night
- Read at least one page in the scriptures every day
- Attend church on a weekly basis
- Provide voluntary service to others

- Use the scriptures as a standard against which to judge their thoughts and behaviors; live in a manner that is consistent with this standard
- When their behaviors do not conform to the scriptures, make an earnest effort to change by striving to bring them into conformance (repentance)

WHAT I PLAN TO TEACH

- The key to becoming a happy person is to learn to live a balanced life. Developing yourself spiritually is an important part of being balanced.
- According to an unknown author, becoming spiritual requires us to "gain victory over ourselves, and to come into communion with the infinite (God). Spirituality impels one to conquer difficulties and acquire more and more strength. To feel one's faculties unfolding, and truth expanding in the soul, is one of life's most sublime experiences."
- Considerable scientific and testimonial research indicates there are many benefits to becoming spiritual in a religious context.
- People who are spiritual have the added dimension of understanding that with God, nothing is impossible. They also recognize that although the world we live in is filled with problems, it is also filled with things we need to overcome them.
- Praying, meditating, reading scriptures and inspirational words on a daily basis, striving to live in conformity with the scriptures, working to overcome our weaknesses, and serving others can help us to become more spiritual and to experience joy.
- Attending church can help us to become more spiritual because it puts us in touch with others who are like-

minded, provides us with encouragement to improve ourselves, and provides opportunities for service.
- Providing voluntary service to others is a reward in itself.
- Use scripture as a standard against which to judge thoughts and behaviors, and live in a manner that is consistent with this standard.
- When your behaviors do not conform to the scriptures, make an earnest effort to change by striving to bring your actions into conformance. That is, when you do things that are contrary to what is outlined in the scriptures, you should strive to overcome these things by feeling sorrow, confessing, and making restitution. For example, if you are unkind to others, you should feel sad about what you did and do something nice to make those you hurt feel better, such as buying them an ice-cream cone or helping them with their chores. This will make both the offender and the person he or she hurt feel better. Doing something nice for the person you hurt will show that you are really sorry. Most importantly, strive not to be unkind again, because this will undo all that you have done. If you do, however, make the same mistake again, go through the same steps to make up for your mistake. Eventually, you will overcome your tendency to hurt others.

HOW I PLAN TO TEACH IT (MY METHODS)

- Explain the purposes and benefits of becoming spiritual.
- Give an account of how spirituality has helped in my life.
- Read an inspirational story like "David and Goliath."
- Watch an inspirational movie like "Chariots of Fire."
- Play inspirational music while everyone quietly mediates. After meditating, listen to everyone who wants to share personal feelings about God.
- Memorize a scripture from the Bible.

- Watch a video like The Ten Commandments (by Cecil B. DeMille), or Disney's The Prince of Egypt.
- Assign children independent reading about a religious topic or a famous religious person and have them report back to the family about what they have learned from their readings.
- Demonstrate how to pray and model regular church attendance.
- Plan and participate in a service project, such as visit a friend in a hospital, bake cookies for a neighbor, or write a letter to grandma.

HOW I PLAN TO FIND OUT IF THEY KNOW AND DO WHAT I WANT THEM TO

- Hold one-on-one interviews using the Progress Tracker to determine what the children know about spirituality and what they intend to do or are doing about it (in accordance with what is described above).

HOW I PLAN TO REINFORCE WHAT I HAVE TAUGHT

- Model church attendance, personal prayer (by holding daily family prayer), striving to live a life that conforms to the scriptures, admitting and overcoming my mistakes.
- Provide encouragement/support when children follow my example.
- Read and discuss a scripture every night before dinner/bedtime.

SAMPLE LESSON PLAN #13
WE BELIEVE IN BEING MEDIA LITERATE

WHAT I WANT THEM TO KNOW

- Electronic media, including television and movies, can have a good or bad influence upon you.
- It is important to use discretion when deciding what to watch.
- Your values and behaviors are influenced by what you see and think about.
- You should not depend on those who produce television and movies to decide what is and is not appropriate for you to watch.
- You should not watch movies or TV programs that do not follow family guidelines.
- Watching television can take you away from other activities that you need to be a healthy person.
- Learning the mechanics and artistry involved in creating TV and movies (script, subtext, lighting, music, casting) can help you better appreciate and evaluate this form of entertainment.

WHAT I WANT THEM TO DO

- Be discriminating in the TV and movies they watch, both in terms of quality and quantity
- Avoid TV and movies that promote values not consistent with family values

WHAT I PLAN TO TEACH

- Our family has specific rules regarding watching TV and movies to protect you morally and spiritually.
- What is good about TV and movies? TV can be used to promote positive values and character traits. The media can draw our attention to problems in society and provide ideas about how to overcome them. The "real" movies, such as documentaries and nature shows, can be educational.
- Many programs sensationalize violence, show sex without consequences, and portray adults who seem to never grow up. These artificial and oftentimes crude depictions of life can convey the idea that violence is an acceptable means of resolving problems, that sex is simply an act of temporary pleasure, that being single is preferable to being married, and that everything is funny when, in fact, just the opposite is true. Most adults do settle down; not everything in life is funny (as is depicted in many sitcoms); not everyone is trim and sexy (nor need they be); marriage and family life are wonderful and much better than the "easy come, easy go" mentality depicted on the big screen.
- Advertisements that attempt to persuade us to buy things we do not need, particularly on credit, can give the false impression that life is a "play now, pay later" proposition.
- It is important to be able to distinguish the difference

between "real" TV and the kind that portrays life as being full of violence, sex, drugs, and cops. TV programs that depict people getting away with things like sex and violence without depicting the consequences are selling a lie. No matter how well the lie is depicted, it is a lie. There are many negative consequences to uncommitted sex, including illegitimate pregnancy, abortion, broken hearts, and sexually transmitted diseases, including HIV/AIDS. In reality, adultery, though often depicted as romantic and commonplace, often leads to divorce, dashed hopes and dreams of children, and a multitude of other problems that can last a lifetime. Every time a real person is killed, family members suffer under the weight of grief, funeral expenses, lost potential income, and on and on. When you watch TV programs and movies that do not show reality, you can develop a false perception of the "real world." Young people who do not have much experience in life may take risks and do things they would not do if they were aware of the many negative consequences associated with the high-risk behavior that is glorified onscreen. They do not realize that even though we can choose what to do with our lives, we have no choice about consequences.

- TV and movie producers would have us follow their guidance on what to watch. They have produced rating systems to help us monitor our viewing habits; however, if they were truly concerned about our well-being, they would not produce promiscuous and violent movies. Do not trust those who promote violent and irresponsible behavior to give you good guidance on what you should or should not watch. For the most part, their main objective is to make money, and they know that, for better or worse, humans are naturally attracted to sex and violence. Hence, they exploit this human tendency, regardless of the consequences, to make money.

- Establish your own TV or movie rating system.
- There are many important and interesting things you can do instead of watching TV: swim, practice a musical instrument, read a book, roller blade, bake cookies, write a letter or write in your journal, do homework, ride your bike, fly a kite, acquire a hobby like making jewelry or pottery, work on an art project, walk the dog or herd the cat, call a friend, shoot baskets, practice fencing or karate, and so on.
- You can learn how to resist the pressure to watch bad movies.
- You can learn what to do when you are with your friends and a movie you are watching turns out to be a bad one.
- A steady diet of violence can make people insensitive to pain, more aggressive, and inclined to perceive a world full of violence.

HOW I PLAN TO TEACH IT (MY METHODS)

- Discuss ways of rating music, TV, and movies.
- Devise a Family Rating System that is consistent with our family values and sets guidelines for when, how much, and what kinds of entertainment are appropriate for our family members.
- Assign kids to watch, analyze, and report on four commercials.
- Assign them to watch, analyze, and report on two movies.
- Assign them to watch, analyze, and report on two sitcoms.
- Make a video using all the basic elements, including music (CD player for background music) and lighting.
- Put together a newscast (which story comes first, which gets told, from whose perspective), a sitcom, a movie, or documentary. Assign different individuals to write,

direct, and produce some form of entertainment that you will later analyze as a family.
- Watch and discuss a video together.
- Watch and discuss a sitcom together. How does the sitcom uphold or go against our family's goals? In many instances, kids talk back to parents, parents are portrayed to be less competent than kids, people are selfish, children are rude to each other, people care more about money than other people, people are dishonest, people have low morals and use crude language.
- Review all points in previous section of the lesson plan.

HOW I PLAN TO FIND OUT IF THEY KNOW AND DO WHAT I WANT THEM TO

- Hold one-on-one interviews using the Progress Tracker to determine what they know and plan to do about media literacy.

HOW I PLAN TO REINFORCE WHAT I HAVE TAUGHT

- Set a good example by only partaking in entertainment that supports our family values.

SAMPLE LESSON PLAN #14
HOW TO CORRELATE AND CALENDAR FAMILY ACTIVITIES

WHAT I WANT THEM TO KNOW

- There are advantages to planning ahead.
- When we plan ahead, things go better.
- We can learn to correlate family activities.

WHAT I WANT THEM TO DO

- Meet with the family on a weekly basis to plan and correlate activities
- Keep a personal calendar (keep on wall for younger children)

WHAT I PLAN TO TEACH

- When we plan ahead, things go better.
- We can plan better activities.
- When we know what is coming up, we can better prepare.

- If we plan ahead and save money, we can participate in exciting family activities, including vacations.
- When we plan ahead, we can avoid last-minute decisions that can be costly and can cause stress and family conflict.
- If we plan ahead, the family can better support you in your individual activities because we will know when and where they are scheduled.
- Each family member should keep a calendar and bring it to our weekly family meeting.
- We will schedule all family activities, school activities, tests and project due dates, etc.
- HOW I PLAN TO TEACH IT (MY METHODS)
- Obtain a large "family" calendar that can be hung in a place where everyone can see it.
- Prior to the meeting, calendar all of our upcoming activities, including a weekly family meeting (when we will correlate family activities and teach a lesson). Also, record a time when we plan to have a weekly outing or activity (like every Saturday afternoon, or the first Saturday of the month, or during dinner out as a family on Thursdays).
- Explain the benefits of keeping a calendar.
- Demonstrate how to manage the calendar.
- Give everyone their own calendar and ask them to list their upcoming activities, including the weekly family meeting and activity/outing.

HOW I PLAN TO FIND OUT IF THEY KNOW AND DO WHAT I WANT THEM TO

- Observe at every weekly family meeting whether or not children are keeping their calendars current.
- Hold one-on-one interviews using the Progress Tracker to

determine if children need help in keeping their calendars current.

HOW I PLAN TO REINFORCE WHAT I HAVE TAUGHT

- Post a family calendar and refer to it every evening to remind everyone what is coming up the next day.
- Set an example by keeping my own calendar current.
- Reward children when they come to family meetings with their calendar current.

SAMPLE LESSON PLAN #15
WE BELIEVE IN SHOWING KINDNESS TO EVERYONE

WHAT I WANT THEM TO KNOW

- Kindness is treating others in a nice way.
- Kindness is an important family value.
- We should be kind to everyone, even people who are mean to us.

WHAT I WANT THEM TO DO

- Practice being kind to others
- Treat others the way they want to be treated
- Encourage other people instead of tearing them down
- Repeat the good things instead of the bad things they know about other people

WHAT I PLAN TO TEACH

- Kindness is treating other people in a nice way by saying nice things to them and doing nice things for them.

- You should practice being kind to everyone, even those people who are not kind to you.
- If someone yells at you, answer him or her in a soft voice. If you yell back, it will only make matters worse.
- When others get to know you, they will treat you like you treat them. Therefore, if you treat other people with kindness, others will eventually treat you the same way. You will have many more friends when you practice kindness, because people like to be around kind people.
- Do not think bad things about other people. Even if they are mean to you, think to yourself, "She must be having a bad day, week, month or year," or "He must be feeling weak today," because rudeness is a weak person's imitation of strength. When you are rude, you are weak, and it does not feel good to be weak.
- When you talk about other people, mention their good points instead of their weaknesses.
- Learn to say kind things to people. Always build people up instead of tearing them down. Never call people names that can hurt their feelings.
- The best way to show kindness is to do nice things for people even when they do not ask you to.
- Take the time to listen carefully when other people talk to you. This is a great way to show you care.

HOW I PLAN TO TEACH IT (MY METHODS)

- Ask everyone for ideas about what they think kindness is.
- Ask how they feel when people treat them rudely. Ask, "Would you rather be around rude people or kind people?" Ask them how they feel when people are kind to them.
- During our family meeting, ask everyone to write down something nice about everyone else in the family. Then

read the responses aloud. Ask how they felt when they heard nice things about themselves
- Explain points made above.
- Make a list of kind words.
- Role-play responding in a kind way to someone who is not kind.
- Write every child a note and tell him or her how great you think he or he is.
- Do a chore for every child and follow up by saying, "I did a kind thing for you today because I love you."
- Post a sign that says, "Our Family Believes in Random Acts of Kindness."

HOW I PLAN TO FIND OUT IF THEY KNOW AND DO WHAT I WANT THEM TO

- Observe how family members treat one another, whether or not they use kind words and do kind deeds,
- Hold one-on-one interviews using the Progress Tracker to determine what they know about the importance of kindness and what they are doing about it.

HOW I PLAN TO REINFORCE WHAT I HAVE TAUGHT

- Model kindness in my daily activities.
- Do something nice for the children when they are not expecting it.
- Leave notes expressing love and appreciation.
- Buy treats or things they like, for no reason at all. (Although gifts are often expected on birthdays and many holidays, they are not expected because a person smiled or said something nice. We will give small gifts and say nice things when the children least expect it.)

SAMPLE LESSON PLAN #16
ACCEPTING DISCIPLINE WITH A GOOD ATTITUDE

WHAT I WANT THEM TO KNOW

- When you disobey family rules we, as loving parents, are obligated to administer discipline.
- When you disobey society's rules, you will be punished.
- Discipline is designed to help you correct the things you do wrong.
- Discipline will be designed to fit the infraction.
- If you constantly disobey the same rule, the disciplinary measures will become more harsh.
- You should comply with discipline with a good attitude and without constant parental supervision.
- Everyone makes mistakes.
- You should strive to learn from your mistakes.

WHAT I WANT THEM TO DO

- Observe all family and societal rules
- When they disobey rules and discipline is administered, they will accept the discipline with a good attitude

- Comply with discipline without constant supervision from parents
- Strive to learn from their mistakes
- Encourage others in the family to obey family rules, and when they are disciplined, willingly comply

WHAT I PLAN TO TEACH

- Discipline is a form of correction that is designed to train and motivate you to obey certain rules. If it is administered fairly and with love, it can help you develop self-control, character, and orderliness. It can also help you learn respect for authority and rules.
- When you disobey family rules, you will be disciplined. This will teach you the importance of obeying your parents and their rules. It should motivate you to do what is expected of you.
- When you disobey society's rules, you will be punished. For example, if you drive too fast you may get a traffic ticket. If you get caught using illegal drugs you will most likely spend time in jail, do community services, pay fines, and report to a probation officer for an extended period of time.
- Discipline is designed to draw attention to the incorrect things you do and motivate you to correct these things.
- In our family, discipline will be designed to fit the infraction.
- If you constantly disobey the same rule, the disciplinary measure will become more harsh.
- You should comply with discipline with a good attitude and without constant parental supervision.
- The following questions will help you recognize the importance of self-monitoring and the commitment of your parents and other adults to help you learn to monitor your behavior and make better choices.

- How do you feel when your parents remind you that you are doing something wrong?
- Do you get mad and try to defend your behavior (even though you know it is wrong)?
- Are you grateful when others attempt to correct you?
- Do you get angry and hold a grudge against those who offer you advice on how to overcome your faults?
- Listen to the following story about the horse and answer the questions to determine how you feel when your actions are corrected by someone who has authority over you.

One of our horses named Dakota developed a serious condition that required twelve daily injections of an antibiotic to save his life. On the second day of Dakota's treatment he ran from me to avoid the painful injections. Because Dakota's continued to resist treatment I decided to lock him in a stall where I could easily access him. Fortunately, Dakota and I survived the twelve day process without serious injury or complications. For several months after receiving treatment, Dakota was very hard to catch and even more difficult to saddle.

- How do think the horse felt about receiving treatment?
- How do you know the horse owner cared about the horse?
- If we compare your disobedience to Dakota's attempts to avoid treatment, how might the actions taken to treat the horse be compared to the actions I take when you are unwilling to cooperate with my rules and requests?
- When I take time to correct you, even if you do not want to be corrected, what does that say about my feelings about you?

Listen to the following hypothetical situation and answer the questions to determine how it relates to discipline.

> *Imagine walking home from school. You see your little brother playing ball in the front yard. The ball goes into the street. You also see a truck coming down the street while your brother starts toward the ball.*

- What would you do?
- What would you say to him after the truck passed?
- What if he became angry with you for correcting him?
- How might we misunderstand our parents when they try to correct us?

When someone illuminates the fact that you are doing something wrong, be humble and thank him or her. Do not hold a grudge. It is true that some people do not correct people in a spirit of love. Forgive them anyway.

We understand that everyone makes mistakes. However, we should strive to learn from and overcome our faults.

HOW I PLAN TO TEACH IT (MY METHODS)

- Define discipline and explain when and why it will be applied in our family.
- Discuss how society applies discipline, and for what reasons.
- Ask the above questions before and after I read the story to determine how the children initially look at discipline and how they feel about it after the story.
- Repeat the explanation of why we apply discipline.
- Encourage them to be humble and realize that discipline is an act of love designed to help rather than hurt them.
- Review the family rules, the purpose of having family rules, and the types of discipline that will be applied if

the rules are violated. Also note that discipline will not be applied until parents have had time to hear what happened and to think about what form of discipline best fits the infraction.
- Show a video that reinforces the benefits of correct discipline.

HOW I PLAN TO FIND OUT IF THEY KNOW AND DO WHAT I WANT THEM TO

- Observe how well each child adheres to rules and accepts discipline.
- Hold one-on-one interviews using the Progress Tracker to determine if children understand the rules and the corresponding consequences and if they are willing to abide by the rules and humbly accept correction.

HOW I PLAN TO REINFORCE WHAT I HAVE TAUGHT

- Model loving discipline by not disciplining until I know all the facts.
- When I make mistakes or am corrected by someone, I will accept the correction with a good attitude.
- Occasionally tell stories about how discipline can help people improve.

SAMPLE LESSON PLAN #17
DEVELOPING PROPER GROOMING HABITS

WHAT I WANT THEM TO KNOW

- People judge you and treat you a certain way based on your physical appearance and hygiene.
- It is important to be your "best self" by keeping yourself clean, well-dressed, and in good mental and physical condition.

WHAT I WANT THEM TO DO

- Adopt and practice good grooming habits

WHAT I PLAN TO TEACH

- Other people judge you based on your appearance and your personal hygiene.
- If you dress in a neat and orderly manner, people (particularly adults) tend to show you more respect.
- You should develop a habit of good grooming by adopting the following habits: 1) maintain good posture,

2) shower or bathe every day, 3) wash your hair at least every other day, 4) wash your entire body with soap, 5) wear deodorant (as a teenager), 6) keep your nails clean and trim, 7) avoid nail-biting, 8) keep your hair trim and neat, 9) keep your leather shoes polished, 10) keep your clothes in good repair (buttons sewed on, tears promptly repaired, generally clean and neat), 11) brush your teeth morning and night, 12) floss your teeth daily, 13) get sufficient exercise, and 14) eat a healthy diet so you can keep your weight at a desirable level.

HOW I PLAN TO TEACH IT (MY METHODS)

- Explain what good grooming is, why it is important, and what we want the children/teenagers to do about it.
- Put together a grooming checklist to hang in the bathroom.
- Show a video that explains the benefits of good grooming and demonstrates examples of good grooming.

HOW I PLAN TO FIND OUT IF THEY KNOW AND DO WHAT I WANT THEM TO

- Observe whether or not children are practicing good grooming habits.
- Hold one-on-one interviews using the Progress Tracker to determine what they know and what they are doing about good grooming habits.

HOW I PLAN TO REINFORCE WHAT I HAVE TAUGHT

- Set an example of good grooming.
- Compliment children when they are well-groomed.
- Conduct follow-up lessons on the importance of good grooming.

SAMPLE LESSON PLAN #18
UNDERSTAND WE ARE WHAT WE EAT

WHAT I WANT THEM TO KNOW

- Eating a balanced diet can help you look, feel, and function better.

WHAT I WANT THEM TO DO

- Eat a low-fat and high-fiber diet
- Limit foods and beverages that are high in calories and low in nutrients

WHAT I PLAN TO TEACH (Obviously, this will change with time as we learn more about what works and what doesn't work in maintaining a healthy weight.)

- The USDA Food Pyramid and the U.S. Dietary Guidelines help us choose healthy foods in the appropriate portions.
- Eating a low-fat diet can help you maintain a healthy weight, become more socially acceptable, feel better

about yourself and the way you look, have more energy, and have more fun. Strive to eat less than 25 grams of fat per day.
- Eating foods that are high in fiber helps regulate your body's metabolism, improves digestion, and helps prevent disease. Strive to eat more than 12 grams of fiber each day.
- Drink at least six 8-ounce glasses of liquid every day, preferably water and milk.
- Limit the candy and carbonated beverages you consume because they are high in calories and low in nutrients.
- Do not drink caffeinated beverages, including caffeinated tea and soda pop.

HOW I PLAN TO TEACH IT (MY METHODS)

- Display and explain the *USDA Back to Basics: All About MyPlate Food Groups*.
- Lecture on the importance of eating low-fat and high-fiber foods.
- Provide each family member a list of low-fat and high-fiber foods.
- Demonstrate how to determine the amount of fat and fiber in different foods (note, we use the Weight Watcher's guide at https://www.weightwatchers.com/us/).
- List high-calorie/low-nutrient foods. Discuss ways of limiting these foods.
- Help children list their favorite low-fat and high-fiber foods, and write a plan that they will follow for one week to track how many fat and fiber grams they consume each day. Also, have them set a goal for limiting the number of high-calorie/low-nutrient foods they eat over the coming week.
- Serve low-fat/high-fiber foods and ask children to

estimate the number of fat and fiber grams in each serving.
- Visibly post in the kitchen the *USDA Back to Basics: All About MyPlate Food Groups.*

HOW I PLAN TO FIND OUT IF THEY KNOW AND DO WHAT I WANT THEM TO

- At the next meeting, have children report on their progress.
- Hold one-on-one interviews using the Progress Tracker to determine if children are eating low-fat/high-fiber foods.

HOW I PLAN TO REINFORCE WHAT I HAVE TAUGHT

- Refer children to the USDA Food Pyramid and the U.S. Dietary Guidelines posted in the kitchen.
- Serve favorite low-fat and high-fiber foods.
- Develop your own personal examples.

SAMPLE LESSON PLAN #19
DEVELOPING PROBLEM SOLVING

WHAT I WANT THEM TO KNOW

- We all experience problems.
- We can learn to solve problems effectively and teach others to do the same.
- Complaining about problems is not an effective way to solve them and can even be counterproductive.
- Life is not fair. Many of the problems we experience are caused by others.
- If we become good at solving problems, we will be highly valued by society and will experience a greater sense of well-being.
- The Serenity Prayer offers guidance to help us solve and accept problems.

WHAT I WANT THEM TO DO

- Accept that everyone has problems
- Adopt and apply a systematic approach to solving problems

WHAT I PLAN TO TEACH

- All families and individuals have problems. It is irrational to think otherwise.
- Problems are a discrepancy between what we want and what we experience.
- Complaining about problems is not an effective way to solve them and can be counterproductive.
- Life is not fair. Many of the problems we experience are caused by others. If we accept these problems as a challenge and work through them, we can become good at solving problems.
- People who are good at solving problems are highly valued by society and experience a greater sense of well-being because 1) they accept the rational idea that all people have problems, 2) they are not afraid of the challenge that problems present, 3) they have learned to effectively solve their problems and thereby reduce the stress that accompanies them, and 4) they have learned to be patient and/or accepting when problems are not readily resolved.
- The Serenity Prayer: God grant me the serenity to accept the things I cannot change, the courage to change the things I can, and the wisdom to know the difference.
- You can learn to solve problems effectively and teach others to do the same. There are many good problem-solving approaches you can use to identify and overcome familial and individual problems. One good approach is to use the Problem Solving Planner, or PSP. This tool has two phases.
- Phase I of the PSP directs you to 1) identify the problem, 2) define it, 3) investigate to determine the causes and possible solutions, 4) decide which causes you will address and which action steps you will take to alleviate

these causes, and 5) establish a schedule for monitoring progress and getting feedback that can be used to improve the strategy. In Phase II you put the information together to make up your intervention strategy. An example of how the PSP can be applied in overcoming the problem of low grades in school is described as follows.

Phase I - Understanding the Problem

Step 1: Assume you want to help your child raise low grades. You expect your child to get As and Bs in school but he or she is getting Cs, Ds, and Fs. Your child has a problem; you have a problem.

Step 2: You define the problem as, "We expect you to get all As and Bs on your report card and you got a D in your Political Systems class. You have a problem. We will help you identify what is causing your problem and what steps you can take to overcome it." (Note that although you have agreed to help identify a strategy for overcoming the problem, you have placed ownership of the problem on your son/daughter.)

Step 3: You talk to your child and your child's Political Systems teacher to determine what is causing the problem. Your child says the reasons why she is not doing well in the class are that she does not like the class, the teacher is boring, and she does not see how the class can help her in the future. On the other hand, the teacher says your child is having difficulties with the class because she does not pay attention to the class lectures, and therefore she does not take good notes which, in turn, means she cannot prepare for the tests. You talk to your child further and discover she has difficulty taking notes because the teacher lectures very fast and she cannot keep up. You ask your daughter if she has any good friends in the class who might be willing to share their notes. You find out that she does not know anyone in the class on a personal level (another potential problem). Because there are still nine weeks left in the class, you talk to the school to find out whether or not your child can be transferred to another Political Systems class. You are told no. You then visit the local library and check out a book on note-taking.

SAMPLE LESSON PLAN #20
LEARNING AND PRACTICING SELF-CONTROL

WHAT I WANT THEM TO KNOW

- You can learn to control yourself.
- You can resist impulses.
- You can resist pressure from others.

WHAT I WANT THEM TO DO

- Delay gratification
- Consciously strive to develop self-control
- Control thoughts and actions

WHAT I WILL TEACH: What it is:

- Self-control is intentionally asserting control over your thoughts and actions to prevent yourself from thinking and doing things that are beyond your familial and personal limits.
- If you practice, you can learn to control the way you talk, the way you look, the way you treat others, the way you

dress, your situation in life, the environments you are in (at least to some extent), your motives, your standards, the way you think (remember that thoughts trigger actions), your urges, your behavior, and YOUR LIFE!

RELEVANT QUOTES:

> "A simple reality which is ignored at a terrible price is that most human misery can be prevented by wise and disciplined living." (Victor Brown)

> "The breakdown of sexual self-control is a big factor in many of the sex-related problems that plague our society, including: rape, sexual promiscuity, pornography, addiction to sex, sexual harassment, the sexual abuse of children, sexual infidelity in marriage, and the serious damage to families many of these problems cause." (Thomas Likona)

> "You can't do wrong and feel right, it's impossible." (Ezra Taft Benson)

SOME PROBLEMS that can arise if you do not have self-control:

EXAMPLE 1: Some people never learn to control themselves. Therefore, even though they get older, they never become responsible. This causes all kinds of problems. For example, some people never learn to control how much they eat. As a result, they eat more food than they need (or the wrong kinds of food) and they become overweight. This does not make them bad people, but it can cause them many problems. For instance, they are not as socially acceptable; they cannot participate in activities that require a person to be in good physical condition; they do not have as much energy; they do not feel good about themselves;

and they can have health problems that result from being overweight.

EXAMPLE 2: Some people never learn to control their thoughts. This is a problem because they do not learn to concentrate on what they are doing. For example, if you are in school and you do not control what you are thinking about, you will not be able to concentrate on what your teacher is saying. This will prevent you from learning what is being taught, and you will not do as well as you could do in your schoolwork.

> *People who are out of control overeat, oversleep, do not study, scream at others, hit others, shoot others, drink and drive, get in car accidents, and so on. If the people in a society are out of control, the society itself is out of control.*

SOME OF THE BENEFITS of having self-control:

- Those who learn to practice self-control are responsible.
- People who are in control of themselves are free to do whatever they choose; those who are out of control are imprisoned by their habits. People who are in control make better students, athletes, artists, teachers, employees, and managers.
- It is not always easy or fun to be in control, but it is worth it.
- It is not much fun to practice playing a musical instrument every day, but it is fun to be able to play music. It is not easy to lift weights or work out every day, but it is worth it to be strong and have an attractive body. It is not that much fun to study, but it is fun to get good grades. It is fun to be in control. If you are in control, you can do anything you decide you truly want to do.
- Not everything that is worthwhile is easy or fun.
- Because your thoughts and feelings (impulses) precede

your actions, learn to control your thoughts. If you have an impulse to do something that you know you should not do, redirect your thinking to something else. Learn a song or memorize a poem, or exercise, or do something that takes your mind off what you know you should not do.
- Put first things first. That is, practice doing hard things before easy ones. For example, do your homework or your chores before you go out to play with your friends. Do not give yourself permission to do fun things until you have taken care of your responsibilities.
- Remind yourself that it is not easy, but it is fun, to be in control.
- Ignore others who tempt you to do things you do not want to do.
- Avoid influences that tempt you to do what you should not or prevent you from doing what you should. For example, do not watch television programs or movies, or listen to music, that tempt you or cause you to think thoughts that lead you astray.
- Do watch TV, read books, and attend activities that encourage you to do the things you want to do.

HOW I WILL TEACH IT (MY METHODS)

- Find out what the children already know by asking questions.
- After I find out, I will describe what I think self-control is.
- Ask one child to read a related quote.
- Ask children what problems can arise if people do not have self-control.
- Relate examples of these problems.
- Ask what the benefits of self-control are.
- Show a video clip of a person exercising self-control. For example, I could show a clip of a great athlete or

performer who focuses on eating well, exercising, and getting enough rest, even when tempted to spend time in less profitable ways. I may show a clip of a person being hit by another person and not returning the blow. The 1982 movie, Gandhi, has several examples of self-control.
- Ask the children to select a movie that has a main character with a lot of self-control, so we can watch the movie together and discuss it.

HOW I PLAN TO FIND OUT IF THEY KNOW AND DO WHAT I WANT THEM TO

- Hold one-on-one interviews using the Progress Tracker to determine what they know about the importance of developing self-control and how well they are improving self-discipline. Ask, "What areas in your life do you control?" (Money? Exercise? Eating? Studying?)

HOW I PLAN TO REINFORCE WHAT I HAVE TAUGHT

- At dinner every evening, we will ask the children to give examples of problems that can result from not having self-control or benefits that can result from having it.
- Visibly post a sign that says, "It's not always easy or fun to be in control, but it's worth it."
- Serve a meal alongside of a favorite dessert. Ask why the meal should be eaten first.
- Make a chart for each child to track how well he or she is improving self-discipline. The chart could have a column indicating what the child plans to do every day to improve his or her self-control and a place to indicate that he or she accomplished the tasks.

SAMPLE LESSON PLAN #21
ACQUIRING THE DIMENSIONS OF HEALTH AND WELL-BEING

WHAT I WANT THEM TO KNOW

- We are multi-dimensional people. We have physical, mental, social, emotional, and spiritual dimensions.
- As healthy people, we strive to live balanced lives by paying attention to our different dimensions.
- There are certain things we need to be happy, healthy, whole people.
- When we are happy and whole people, we can be more loving and supportive family members.

WHAT I WANT THEM TO DO

- Write a self-improvement plan that addresses all of the dimensions we discuss
- Apply the plan for two weeks

WHAT I PLAN TO TEACH

- All people are multi-dimensional beings: social, physical,

intellectual, emotional, spiritual. (See the description of the five dimensions of well-being at the end of this lesson.)
- We all have needs in these areas.
- These needs must be satisfied to ensure that we have good health and well-being.
- If you are not whole, then you cannot reach your full potential in contributing to the overall well-being of the family.
- There is a positive relationship between your overall well-being and the extent to which your needs are satisfied in your social, physical, emotional, intellectual, and spiritual dimensions.
- The relationship between needs and personal well-being is cumulative. That is, if your needs are met on a consistent basis in these areas, you will be healthier and happier (over time) than you would be otherwise. For example, if you hope to be physically fit, you must engage in aerobic exercise on a regular basis. If you do not exercise aerobically on a regular basis, your conditioning will not improve but diminish over time.
- The relationship between your well-being and having your needs met in these areas is also synergistic, which means the combined effect of consistently meeting your needs (in the various dimensions of your being) is greater than the effect of only working on one or two areas at a time. This is due to the interrelationships among these dimensions. For example, a sedentary person who begins exercising on a regular basis experiences an improvement in both mental and physical health.
- We challenge you to write a self-improvement plan and implement the plan for two weeks. The plan should state an action that you will take each day to meet your needs in each of the five areas. For example, you might decide to: 1) (physical) walk one mile every evening, 2)

(intellectual) read one chapter of a good book, 3) (emotional) spend 10 minutes relaxing, 4) (social) say hi to five people you do not know, and 5) (spiritual) pray in the morning and at night.
- If every person in our family consistently strives to improve in these five areas, we will establish and maintain a balance in our lives that will make us more loving and supportive family members. It will also help each of us live to our full potential.

You will be smarter, stronger, better looking, you will feel better, and, as the U.S. Army commercials put it, you will "be all you that you can be." Most importantly, the overall quality of your life will improve.

To illustrate our point more fully, I offer an analogy from a television commercial aired several years ago, sponsored by the people who produce Frahm Oil Filters. In this commercial, a mechanic holds up an oil filter that costs less than $10 and, pointing to the filter, explains the importance of using a good filter and changing your filter on a regular basis. The mechanic ends his spiel by saying, "Pay me now or pay me later," at which point he turns and points to an automobile up on a lift that is obviously getting a major overhaul. The commercial's message is that a consumer can pay a minimal amount on a regular basis by getting an oil change every X-thousand miles and avoid paying a much greater price later on. We believe this principle of "pay me now or pay me later," when applied to the concept of health and well-being, serves to illustrate the importance of consistently taking preventive actions. Accordingly, we will now apply this principle to each of the dimensions of well-being.

HOW I PLAN TO TEACH IT (MY METHODS)

- Ask, "Do you think a person who is physically healthy is always happy?"
- Provide examples of people who are physically healthy, but who have other health problems (i.e., intellectual, mental, social, or spiritual problems).
- Make all of the above points.
- Have each person write a plan to do something every day for two weeks in each of the five areas.
- Assign them all to report back in two weeks on their self-improvement activities.
- Have everyone make and display posters that encourage family members to stick with their self-improvement goals.
- Make a video featuring family members testifying to the benefits of meeting their needs across the five dimensions.
- Make a "Let's Get High-5" poster.

HOW I PLAN TO FIND OUT IF THEY KNOW AND DO WHAT I WANT THEM TO

- Hold one-on-one interviews using the Progress Tracker to determine what they are doing to meet their needs in the five dimensions.
- Observe behavior and encourage children to use the family posters for encouragement.
- Listen to their reports and view their posters.

HOW I PLAN TO REINFORCE WHAT I HAVE TAUGHT

- Write and implement my own self-improvement plan.
- Share my experiences with my self-improvement plan at each family meeting for the next two weeks.

- Take part in the family video.
- Post the "Let's Get High-5" poster.
- Share stories about individuals who have made major changes for the better.

SAMPLE LESSON PLAN #22
PRACTICING SELF-DIRECTED CHANGE

WHAT I WANT THEM TO KNOW

- Our family values encompass self-directed change.
- Engaging in self-directed change is important.
- We can engage in self-directed change by using the Personal Enhancement Planner (PEP).

WHAT I WANT THEM TO DO

- Make a change using the Personal Enhancement Planner (PEP)

WHAT I PLAN TO TEACH

- Our family values self-improvement.

"No man can run away from weakness. He must eventually either defeat it or perish. And if that is so . . . why not now, and where you stand?" (Robert Louis Stevenson)

"A simple reality, which is ignored at a terrible price, is that most human misery can be prevented by wise and disciplined living." (Victor Brown)

- You should continually try to improve yourself by identifying and overcoming weaknesses and by setting goals to accomplish things in your life that will make you a better and more capable person. This will enable you to live to your full potential.
- There is a process that can help you improve called the Personal Enhancement Planner.
- Using this process can make self-directed change easier and fun.

HOW I PLAN TO TEACH IT (MY METHODS)

- Ask the children why change is important, what changes they have made, and what changes they would like to make.
- Tell story about an individual who has made considerable changes in spite of opposition.
- Read quotes and lecture on points made above.
- Review the PEP with an example.
- Ask everyone to select something he or she wants to change about himself or herself and to complete a PEP before the next lesson.
- Ask them to go over their change plan at the next family meeting.

HOW I PLAN TO FIND OUT IF THEY KNOW AND DO WHAT I WANT THEM TO

- Hold one-on-one interviews using the Progress Tracker to determine what they know about the importance of change and how to do it systematically.

- Observe children's behavior to determine whether or not they have incorporated the PEP principles into their lives.

HOW I PLAN TO REINFORCE WHAT I HAVE TAUGHT

- Post the above quotes where everyone can see them. Talk about the quotes and what it means to change.
- Set an example of self-directed change and talk about my own progress with the PEP.

ATTACHMENT
THE PERSONAL ENHANCEMENT PLANNER

A) DETERMINE WHAT YOU WANT TO CHANGE.

Self-Improvement requires changing your behavior by either 1) adding a positive behavior like exercise, or 2) eliminating a negative behavior like oversleeping. To begin self-improvement, select the behavior you want to change. Evaluate the behavior to ensure the change you plan to make is consistent with your personal standards of right and wrong. If the change requires you to go against your personal standards, then select another behavior to work on. If the behavior does fit, and if it "feels like it's the right thing," go on to the next step.

B) MAKE A COMMITMENT TO YOURSELF BY WRITING A CHANGE GOAL.

I will (describe the behavior you plan to add or eliminate)
_____
_____
on or before (date by which you will have maintained this change for at least 21 days)_____.

I will begin preparing for this change on_____.
I will have completed my preparation by_____.
I will begin changing on (date)_____.

C) PREPARE TO CHANGE.

List the things you need to begin and maintain the change. These items include obtaining information (from a credible source), skills, resources (equipment, food, books), permission, etc. Also, list where or from whom you will get these things, and when you will get them. If possible, interview someone, read a book about someone, or watch a movie about someone who made a similar change.

- WHAT DO I NEED?
- WHERE OR FROM WHOM WILL I GET WHAT I NEED?
- WHEN WILL I GET THESE THINGS?

D) DEVELOP YOUR FIRST PLAN FOR CHANGE.

List the steps (small, realistic, achievable) for improvement. Also indicate when you will take these steps (e.g., several times a day, daily, or weekly).

- WHAT I WILL DO?
- WHEN I WILL DO IT?

E) GET SUPPORT FOR CHANGE.

Although the change process is ultimately your responsibility, it can be very helpful to get support from others. Ask one or more people to help you improve. Those who agree to participate should read and sign your improvement strategy.

1. I (name of supporter)_____,

agree to provide support and encouragement to (your name) _____, in his or her efforts to make the change described above. My support will include: _____.

1. I (name of supporter) _____, agree to provide support and encouragement to (your name)_____, in his or her efforts to make the change described above. My support will include:_____.

F) PLAN TO REWARD YOURSELF WHEN YOU MAKE CHANGES.

Rewarding your changes can help you maintain the change. Develop a list of rewards (that are inexpensive and unrelated to food or drugs/alcohol) that you can treat yourself to upon completing each step in your improvement process. Indicate when you will get rewards and under what conditions.

G) VISUALIZE AND LIST THE BENEFITS OF MAKING THIS CHANGE.

Visualizing the benefits (positive outcomes) you expect to gain from making this change will motivate you and help you to remain focused on what you want to accomplish. List these benefits here.

H) VISUALIZE AND LIST THE NEGATIVE CONSEQUENCES OF NOT MAKING THIS CHANGE.

Visualizing the negative outcomes you could face if you do not make this change will motivate you and help you to remain focused on what you do want to accomplish. List these possible negative outcomes here.

I) ANTICIPATE AND LIST THE OBSTACLES TO MAKING THIS CHANGE, AND WHAT YOU CAN DO TO OVERCOME THEM.

Anticipating and developing strategies to overcome obstacles can help you avoid setbacks. List thoughts, behaviors, or excuses that may be barriers to making this change. Also, list external barriers (people, places, things) that may stand in the way of your improvement.

J) DETERMINE AND LIST THOSE THINGS IN YOUR LIFE YOU THAT YOU NEED TO ALTER ABOUT YOURSELF OR YOUR ENVIRONMENT TO MAKE THE CHANGE.

K) WRITE A DAILY ROUTINE FOR CHANGE.

Every day, begin your self-improvement process by doing the following:

1) Visualize the benefits you will get from changing, and the negative consequences if you do not change.
2) Review barriers you may encounter and strategies you will use to overcome them.
3) Review the steps listed in your PEP change strategy and then list those steps you will take action on today (you can list these items on a 3x5 Daily Action Card you can carry with you throughout the day).
4) Follow through consistently and repetitively on the steps you listed on your Daily Action Card.
5) After the change process begins, become aware of unforeseen things that impede your progress; record these as they come up, along with strategies for countering them.
6) When faced with barriers, counter them.
7) Track your progress by keeping a daily log where you

record your daily successes, failures and strategies for overcoming them, insights and lessons learned, and so on

(EMPHASIZE YOUR SUCCESSES); if your improvement plan is not working, make appropriate modifications until you "get it right"; successful change may require a number of modifications in your approach.

Sample Family Plan #2 Using the POG			
Area of Focus: Children's Chores			
List Things You Want to Plan under this Area	Describe What You Want Done	Describe Who Will Do How Much of What, by When, and Where **	Record When and How You Will Follow Up on Action Items
Wash dinner dishes	Take clean dishes out of dishwasher and put them away. Clean off table, rinse off all dirty dishes, put dishes in dishwasher, put soap in dishwasher, and turn on dishwasher.	Dad on Saturday and Sunday, Josh on Monday and Tuesday, Nicholas on Wednesday and Thursday, Mom on Friday	Every evening, before 9 p.m., all dishes must be done or you get an additional day added to your dish schedule.
Vacuum main floor	Vacuum all carpets on the main floor.	Josh will do this every Saturday morning.	Mom or Dad will follow up to determine completeness before 10 a.m. on Saturday.
Vacuum upstairs	Vacuum all carpets upstairs.	Nichole will do this every Saturday morning.	Dad will follow up to determine whether the task is completed on time.

Sample Family Plan #2 Using the POG			
Mow and trim lawn	Mow the front, back, and side yards. Use a bag on mower and place clippings in mulch pile. Trim around the entire house, including the deck and sidewalks.	Josh will do this every Saturday (unless it rains, in which case the first dry day after Sunday) from May 1 through October 1. Other times as needed.	Mom or Dad will check to see if the lawn is mowed. The lawn must be mowed before leaving 10:00 a.m. on Saturday.
Clean upstairs bathrooms	Use cleaning solution to clean the tub and toilet. Use separate clean rag on each. Use a third rag to clean sink and mirrors. Mop the tile floors with floor-cleaning solution.	Jordan will do this every Saturday morning.	This bathroom must be cleaned before 10 a.m. every Saturday morning. Mom and Dad will follow up. You may not leave the house or have friends over until this chore is completed.

**Note: If for some reason you can't do your assigned chores, please make arrangements with another family member to do them for you.

ABOUT THE AUTHOR

Galen Cole, PhD, MPH, LPC, NCC, ABCP, WCPC (www.galencole.com), is a master of public health, licensed and board certified professional counselor, nationally certified counselor, nationally certified hypnotherapist, and an American Board Certified Psychotherapist. He has also received the designation as a World Certified Psychotherapist (WCPC) by the World Council of Psychotherapy in Vienna.

Galen's private practice consists largely of treating high conflict couples and adult clients referred with a history of trauma, mood problems, and/or anxiety conditions. In addition to relying heavily on evidence-based couples and individual therapies, Galen has been recognized for his innovations around an emerging "3rd Wave CBT" psychotherapy known as Life Script Restructuring, which is described in his book by the same title (www.lifescriptrestructuring.com).

He has also been recognized for his innovations in the areas of Trauma-Informed Mindful Cognitive Behavioral Therapy (TI-MCBT)) which has resulted in a trademarked algorithm that is central to understanding and applying the "4th Wave of TI-MCBT." Galen has taught counseling psychology, equine assisted mental health, behavioral and evaluation research, and a number of other counseling and health-related courses at the university level. He's been on the undergraduate and/or graduate faculty at Northern Arizona University, Arizona State University, Pennsylvania State University, and Emory University.

Galen has extensive experience practicing what he teaches, including working on staff and as a consultant at numerous clinics, hospitals, and community based organizations; consulting on a number of popular television series (e.g., The Young and the Restless, Private Practice, The Big C, 90210, Chasing Life, Hostages) — He is the psychotherapist on the 7th and 8th seasons of the popular TLC reality show "The Seven Little Johnstons." Dr Cole has served as the Executive Director of two different 501(c)3 Foundations, worked as an Associate Director of the county public health department in Phoenix, Arizona; and worked for 23 years as a research psychologist, behavioral scientist, and director of research, evaluation, and strategic communication activities in various centers, institutes, and offices at the U.S. Centers for Disease Control and Prevention (CDC) in Atlanta, Georgia. In 2003, Galen was appointed by the Governor of Georgia to serve on the Georgia Human Resources (DHR) Board. In this capacity he served as chair of the DHR committee that provided policy guidance to the state Division of Mental Health, Developmental Disabilities, and Addictive Diseases. After leaving CDC in 2014, Galen took a position as a Senior Mental Health Strategist and Thought Leader at the American Institutes for Research (AIR), headquartered in Washington, D.C. In this position he lead the development of AIR's vision and creative strategies to address the mental health needs of the nation. Galen has served on numerous local, regional, and national boards of directors, including the Board of Professional Counselors at the American Psychotherapy Association. He recently served as President of the Georgia Association of Licensed Professional Counselors. In addition to his private practice, Galen is currently the CEO of the Alive and Well Foundation (www.aliveandwellfoundation.org). He also currently travels throughout the U.S. conducting intensive continuing education workshops on "Cognitive Behavioral Therapy Techniques for Everyday Clinical Practice," on behalf of PESI (pesi.com). Galen has been a trainer and consultant in the Central Asian Republics, Nigeria, China, Thailand, Kenya, Switzerland, Australia, Peru, Germany, Uganda, and the Middle East, where he has consulted and conducted trainings with the Palestinian Health Authority, the Israeli Ministry of Health, and many other NGOs. He has also provided technical support to a number of prominent international organizations, including the United Nations Children's Fund (UNICEF); the Pan American Health Organization (PAHO); the World Bank; Hollywood, Health and Society (HH&S); and the World Health Organization (WHO). Galen has published numerous books and scientific papers, and made presentations at conferences and training seminars across the world. In recognition of his many accomplishments, Galen has received distinguished alumni awards from two of the universities he attended. In 2020 he was designated as an Expert Faculty Lecturer in the "Best of the Best" series sponsored by the American College of Psychology (https://acpsy.org). He and his wife Priscilla have been married since 1975 and are the parents of 5 adult children, and 1 foster child who is still navigating her teenage years.

Printed in Great Britain
by Amazon